family garden

designing a garden for
relaxation, entertaining and play

RICHARD KEY

conran
OCTOPUS

For my wife Ruthie,

and our three boys, Jimmy, Charlie and Tom

First published in 2000 as *Outdoor Living* by
Conran Octopus Limited
a part of Octopus Publishing Group
2–4 Heron Quays
London E14 4JP
www.conran-octopus.co.uk

This paperback edition published in 2003

British Library Cataloguing-in-Publication Data
A catalogue record for this book is available from the
British Library

ISBN 1 84091 335 5

Colour origination by Sang Choy International,
Singapore
Printed and bound in China

commissioning editor: Stuart Cooper

senior editor: Helen Woodhall

assistant editor: Alexandra Kent

copy editor: Paula Hardy

executive art editor: Alison Barclay

designer: Karen Bowen

picture researcher: Julia Pashley

illustrator: Carolyn Jenkins

visualiser: Jean Morley

production: Suzanne Bayliss

indexer: Helen Snaith

author's acknowledgments

Many thanks to Stuart Cooper who presented me with the
opportunity to write this book for which I am extremely grateful.
My thanks to Helen Woodhall for all her hard work, and to Alex
Kent for her calmness and patience as we approached the deadline;
Alison Barclay for inspired design; Julia Pashley for untiring picture
research and for finding such wonderful locations,
and to Ruthie, as always, for everything.

A special thank you to everyone who allowed us to photograph their
amazing gardens for the case studies and who supplied me with
such valuable information.

Finally, I would like to thank those garden designers throughout the
world who, through their inspirational treatment of the outdoor
space, continue to enrich the lives of all of us.

publisher's acknowledgments

The publisher would like to thank Nicola Collings for design
assistance.

CONTENTS

INTRODUCTION

Gardens are for families to enjoy outdoor living, a natural extension of the home where relatives and friends are in close contact with each other and with nature. The garden really is an outdoor room, often the largest that any of us will ever own.

Today's gardens have become multifunctional. Lawns may be for games but also for picnics and parties, paved terraces can be used for sunbathing in the day and supper parties in the evening, and treehouses may be for play or alternatively an author's retreat. The garden is far more than a place to grow flowers, fruit and vegetables. It has become somewhere to escape from hectic lifestyles, a place to relax and play games, to entertain friends and strengthen family bonds – an environment designed to lift your spirits and improve the quality of your life.

Gone are the days when there were 'no go' areas for children and striped lawns that were to be admired but never played on. Gardens have become accessible to everyone, full of interesting spaces to be shared and secret corners to be enjoyed, not shrines of horticultural excellence to be entered with fear and trepidation. When referring to gardens, the terms 'formal' and 'informal' no longer strictly apply. They are more relevant in an historical context than in a a contemporary garden where the terms 'order' and 'disorder' are more applicable.

Family gardens need a fair degree of order in the organisation of space – paved areas to sit on and firm pathways leading to utility areas. Without this order, gardens can soon become chaotic, with seating set in a jungle of foliage and overgrown grass while pathways turn to mud which is then trampled through the house. Having said this, a little disorder in a family garden does not hurt and, in fact, it should probably be actively encouraged as it can provide a comfortable 'lived in' feeling. Lawns do not have to be cut bowling green short and edged razor sharp but the grass can be left a bit longer. Mosses growing in the joints of paving are more pleasing than a terrace that has been jet-washed clean, while self-sown feverfew and forget-me-nots covering bare soil where they are not intended to be are fine.

To some people, unfamiliar with garden design, there is a belief that gardens just happen without any planning. While it is true that many gardens do develop in this unsatisfactory piecemeal fashion, the most successful gardens are achieved through a careful analysis of the site, individual requirements and personal taste. Above all, be comfortable with your garden and take care at the planning stage to create an area that is right for you.

If you are dissatisfied with your garden avoid the temptation to make impulsive changes: instead, take a step back and look at the bigger picture to ensure that the changes you do make will not be to the detriment of other parts of your garden. Gardens do not need to look designed, they just need to look right, to look comfortable and practical, to have style without making a grand statement.

Gardens and families are constantly changing and evolving. It is this dynamism that comes together to form the very core of this book. While some books deal with the art of garden design, focusing on construction details and planting plans, this book concentrates on gardens for people and their families.

LEFT: Even gardens designed for minimum maintenance require occasional tending, although the grasses which have been planted in this Australian garden leave little room for weeds to grow.

LEFT BELOW: In the daytime, roof terraces benefit from big bright skies and fantastic panoramic views, while at night there are starlit skies and the sparkling lights of a city skyline. The parapet wall with toughened glass panels around this terrace allows uninterrupted views and acts as a safety barrier.

OPPOSITE: The splendid pavilion in this garden can be used equally well for entertaining friends or for relaxing in the cool shade while watching the more energetic members of the family charging around the tennis court.

design for **outdoor living**

DESIGN *for* OUTDOOR LIVING

Any outdoor space can be turned into a useful living

ABOVE: Overhead beams
and trellis with climbing
plants gently filter light
into this shaded and
intimate sitting area. The
timber beams add to the
privacy of this space by
obscuring views from
neighbouring windows.

Planning a garden is all about organising the space available in the best possible way for people, plants and structures alike. All the functions of your garden must be considered in a practical way in order to give sufficient room for all the family's outdoor activities, many of which, in a small garden, may need to share the same space. A well-planned garden can be truly multi-functional, incorporating lawns and paved terraces to be used for relaxing, cooking and eating alfresco and for a vast array of children's games.

OPPOSITE BELOW: The garden at the rear of this tall terraced house has been designed superbly to integrate indoor and outdoor. A balcony looks over a contemporary conservatory in which supper parties can be enjoyed in comfort under starlit skies, while a stone patio with pots and timber furniture provide for entertaining outdoors.

LEFT: A cool and tranquil seating area has been created in this roof-top garden. Trees and plants hide nearby buildings, but also frame a stunning view over the city. The table and chairs offer a shaded retreat from the bright sunlight, while the long lines of the timber slats help to create a visual illusion that the garden is larger than it really is.

space for all the family to enjoy.

When you start to list all the functions of your garden try to think about appearance and practicalities. If there is no hidden area for a washing line, for example, then create one – a trellis panel with climbing plants works well, taking up little room but adding interest and height to the garden. Children love to play with sand and water but siting a sandpit next to an outside tap is not a good idea if you want to avoid a swamp; allowing the children to walk a few metres around the garden with buckets of water may be more practical. Plan ahead for low maintenance, too; a brick edge around the lawn will eliminate the need for laborious trimming. Better still, make the edge a brick path so that young children can have a circular trike track while you have access around the garden on a hard surface. This

makes maintenance of surrounding beds far easier and it also allows you to stroll around your garden, taking in different views, making it a far more enjoyable place.

There is no doubt that gardens can lift the spirit and change your mood as you pass from one area to another. These changing moods or atmospheres can be planned for by introducing different styles into different areas: a shaded arbour, a barbecue terrace and a games lawn are all spaces that will have their own individual atmospheres.

The style of your garden will inevitably be influenced by your personality and individual taste just like the interior design of your home. In this way the garden, which is an extension of your living space, will be linked visually with the rooms in your house. Your garden can be whatever you

want it to be; look at books and magazines for inspiration but do not pick out a plan for a square garden simply because that is the shape of your plot, and avoid designing on a whim of fashion. Fads will come and go but to copy outright may be shortsighted and leave you feeling dissatisfied after a couple of years. Gardens that are designed to be totally incongruous with their surroundings can, on occasion, be successful but they require great skill in execution. However, you may want to add a refreshing surprise to one corner of your garden by introducing something that is out of character. This juxtaposition of different styles can introduce a real sense of vitality to the garden and need not be over complicated, for example, a contemporary sculpture set among old-fashioned roses or wild flowers.

PLANNING YOUR SPACE

Building a new garden can be an exciting project but it can also be expensive, so it really is worthwhile taking your time at the planning stage. To plan the garden you will need to make a lot of lists, starting with all the requirements of the family, both young and old, and not forgetting the pets. Consider paved areas for family meals, sunbathing or even a table tennis table, and for how many such an area would need to cater when everyone is sitting down together to eat. Will you want water in the garden and if so should this be a safe water feature or are the children old enough for an open pool? Think about games and whether you need a flat area of lawn. Do you really need a swimming pool or would it be too hard to justify the cost and the amount of room that it takes up?

It is easy to overlook the more mundane aspects of a garden and get carried away with the exciting parts, but your list needs to be thorough and cover everything. Where will you store all the garden furniture and children's toys? Do you need a shed or will you make do with the garage even though

ABOVE: The importance of a garden sitting comfortably in its surroundings is demonstrated well in this coastal garden. The colour of the stone paving tones beautifully with the sandy beach, while the bright sunny skies are echoed in the blue painted wall built to provide shelter from sea breezes.

LEFT: Gardens contain many elements including patio areas for family meals and, when the children are old enough, perhaps an area of water like this raised pool.

Your requirements

List all your needs for the garden including those of your children and pets before preparing a design.

*

Consider paved areas for access and outdoor entertaining.

*

Is ornamental water a priority or a luxury to add in at a later stage?

*

What play equipment do you need and where will you store it?

*

An area of lawn is essential in most gardens for games and picnics but choose a tough cultivated turf to withstand the wear-and-tear.

*

If you like to barbecue then a simple portable barbecue may be all that you need, but where do you store it? You could build your own and include storage cupboards and an integral seat.

*

Utility areas can be an eyesore so think long and hard about whether you really need a shed, greenhouse and compost bin.

*

What about the pets? Do you need kennels and hutches? Is there any shade in the garden or do you need to introduce some? This may mean planting trees to keep rabbit hutches cool or for dogs to lie under in the hot summer sun.

*

Do you need a washing line? If so, then a retractable line is a neat solution as it coils away when not in use.

RIGHT: The quirky, spiral topiary is striking, particularly as it sits on a traditional lawn with shrub borders forming a surprising focal point which brings this large garden to life. The blue chairs also add to the sense of dramatic contrast in this garden.

the car will have to stay outside all year? Most of us can remember the taste of home-grown vegetables but are you really going to get stuck into a vegetable plot and all the work that it will entail – perhaps a small corner for runner beans will suffice? List the types of plants that you like, bearing in mind maintenance and that the plants will have to withstand the rigours of family life. When you have completed your list of requirements, just stop and think if there is something that you have always wanted in a garden – a cool arbour, a bubbling stream or simply a favourite plant.

Then think about the atmosphere. A change in style will alter the atmosphere of any area of the garden. With different planting and alternative features a peaceful, secret garden with a great depth of cool green foliage, hidden corners and a still

pool can be transformed into a warm vibrant place full of Mediterranean colours, fragrant herbs and splashing water. But special atmospheres can also be produced by something simple, such as the fragrance of a flower remembered from childhood.

When something has style, whether it is a building, a car or a well-cut suit, it is due to good design. With good design, the end product becomes more than purely functional and fit for its intended purpose. In addition to this everything else is right: the shapes, the proportions and the lines all work in perfect harmony. This is equally applicable to gardens where there is the added influence of a sense of place, a feeling that the garden looks just right in its surroundings and sits comfortably with the house. For this to work, the garden needs to be designed in a particular style

that suits its location, whether it is a country cottage garden full of homely charm or a chic urban roof terrace.

The final question must always be the budget. This can be a tricky one to answer as although you may have a figure in mind, you may not know what the costs of paving and plants really are. Another consideration will be whether you intend to do all of the work yourselves or whether part of the budget should be allocated to paying landscape contractors. It may be sensible at this stage to plan the garden that is right for you and then cost it out rather than be too restrained by a budget at this early stage. You can then find ways to make it work, for example, by staggering the work over a period of time while funds build up or else by changing materials to those which are cheaper but still provide the same effect.

ASSESSING THE PLOT

The second stage of the planning process is to make a thorough assessment of the site to see what is already there. This will involve carrying out a simple site survey to show the position of the house and the boundaries together with a record of any existing planting. You will also need to note any changes of level such as existing steps, slopes or hollows. Measuring a small garden is a fairly straightforward task; however, larger plots may prove more tricky, especially if there are a lot of existing trees and awkward changes of level. In this instance it may be wise to enrol the help of a garden designer or surveyor as having an accurate plan of the site is essential.

Make a checklist of all the information that you will need to show on your plan. This list should include measurements around the house (indicating doors and windows), boundary walls and fences, their heights and the position of any gates. Indicate all slopes and steps and use direction arrows to show the best and the poorer views. Make a note of the compass points on your plan, as this will remind you which parts of the garden are the sunniest and which are in shade at certain times of the day. Mark on your plan any existing trees and shrubs, noting down their size and whether they are worth keeping or not.

The planting may give you a clue as to what will grow well in your garden but you should check the soil to be sure. Garden centres sell simple pH kits that will show whether the soil is acid or alkaline; this is essential information, as certain plants such as rhododendrons will not tolerate an alkaline soil so it would be pointless trying to grow them unless your soil was acid.

All this information should be recorded on a simple scaled plan to build up a picture of the whole garden. It is also a good idea to take a set of photographs and pin them next to your plan when you are designing. This will help you remember certain corners of the garden and it may even show up views, both good and bad, that you had not previously appreciated.

LEFT: Stone steps lead down to an enclosed eating area with a rugged stone table. All elements of the design share the same strength and character of the exposed, underlying rock.

Site checklist

Before planning your new garden you will need to draw up a simple site plan. This should illustrate the ground-floor plan of your house, garage and any outbuildings complete with windows, doors, downpipes and drains. Mark on the boundaries of your plot, indicating the height of walls and fences and how they are constructed.

*

Mark up changes of level in your garden. These may be slopes in the lawn or existing steps in a path or terrace.

*

Use a compass to determine the orientation of your garden as this will tell you which areas are in the sun and which are in cool shady corners.

*

Existing trees and shrubs need to be recorded with a note to describe their condition and size. Mature trees can cast a lot of shade so be sure to record a measurement for the spread of the branches.

*

Make a simple check on the soil condition to see if it is sandy or a heavy clay, and whether there are excessively wet areas that need draining or may be suitable for bog plants. A pH testing kit will measure the acidity or alkalinity of the soil which will determine what plants you can grow.

*

Finally, make a note of any good views that you would like to enhance and any poor views you need to conceal.

LEFT: Interest and movement are created here by shrubs and small trees which also soften the boundaries in this garden and obscure the path which leads past the patio and to the stables which lie beyond.

ABOVE: Making use of the vertical elements in a garden is important where space is limited. In this urban garden the pergola creates shade and interest while plants are grown up the walls, leaving more room for play areas below.

TOP: A well-organised utility area can look good, too. This log store and flowering wigwam of beans make a fine composition.

ABOVE: A shady bower draws the eye towards a place to sit and rest in this decorative kitchen garden.

STARTING TO DESIGN

Once you have completed the survey you can begin the enjoyable process of design. Try to think laterally and turn negatives into positives; just because an old shed is in a certain position does not mean that it has to stay there, it could be moved to a better location in order to open up a view. Steep grassy banks can be turned into practical steps and a damp shady corner of the lawn may be just right for ferns and other shade-loving plants.

Builders will always give you a patio outside the living room but that may not be ideal; a better position which enjoys more sunshine and has a better view may be further away from the house. If your garden lacks shade then you could provide some by including a pergola or an arbour covered with climbers. And what about the old greenhouse? Do you really need it? It takes up a lot of space and is positioned in the sunniest spot in the garden; what is more, it has only ever been used as a store and will stand little chance once the footballs start flying. So get rid of it and plan for what you really want rather than planning around objects simply because they are already there.

DRAWING PLANS

Begin drawing up the scheme using your survey as the base plan. Superimpose your ideas on top of this using overlays of tracing paper. At this stage there is no need for any great detail so use a soft pencil to produce a bold and simple design. Designing a family garden is all about organising space for paved terraces, lawns and utility areas and linking them together in a practical yet stylish way.

Plan each space so that there is sufficient room; ensure that all your family can sit down around the table and that the lawn areas are big enough for games but not so large that there is little room for the softening structure of plants. Show all the areas as different zones on your plan and work up the drawing until you are comfortable that each zone is the right size. Normally, if it looks right on paper then it will be all right on the ground.

You can now step up the detail to include paths, slopes and steps to show how the areas of the garden are linked together. Plan pathways that lead around the garden rather than just to the shed and back. This will introduce movement, resulting in a far more interesting outdoor room. There may be some direct access, perhaps from the terrace to the lawn, whereas other areas such as the utility or vegetable plot may be separated from the lawn by a hedge or a dividing screen of trellis panels.

As the plan progresses and the details increase you may feel the need for some professional guidance. All the homework has been done, your requirements are listed

LEFT: This well-designed alcove bench will seat many people without the storage problem and clutter from chairs.

BELOW: Raised beds and built-in seats can save floor space and can also, as this stone bench shows, become works of art.

and a survey plan has been drawn. You know what you want but producing a detailed plan that covers all your needs in a functional and imaginative way can be difficult. In the United Kingdom, the Society of Garden Designers produces a list of experienced accredited designers, covering all areas of the country, who would be able to provide this help. A professional garden designer will not only be able to take a fresh look at the garden but will also provide a depth of experience that could prevent costly errors and so result in savings far in excess of any design fee.

FINAL DETAILS

If you do proceed with the plan yourself, then once you are satisfied with the layout of the garden you can move on to the elements that will add interest and atmosphere. Introducing divisions between areas of the garden will create a series of outdoor rooms – maybe you want to create a space where children can play in their own secret world while adults enjoy a quiet corner to read or sit in the sun. A good trick is to soften the boundaries with shrubs so that they disappear in a depth of planting, visually making the extent of your garden limitless. Even the smallest of gardens can be visually enlarged simply by leading a pathway behind planting or by introducing a screen so that the whole garden is not seen at once.

LEFT: The strong directional lines of the brick path lead towards the stone sculpture which, framed under the leafy archway, forms a powerful focal point in this garden. The brightly coloured roses lining the path in the foreground help to make the shadowy alcove around the sculpture even more mysterious and intriguing.

OPPOSITE LEFT: Framing views into different parts of the garden can often be more rewarding than seeing the whole picture at once. The 'window' set into this wall captures only a glimpse of the garden, enticing you to explore further.

OPPOSITE RIGHT: The framework of trellis and overhead beams creates dappled shade over this quiet sitting area. The trelliswork allows glimpses into the large garden beyond while the opening on to the lawn neatly frames the buildings on the distant skyline.

Design tips

Without focal points gardens can be dull and static places. Elements like a small water feature or an attractive arbour will lead the eye and focus attention. The focus can even be on something which lies outside the area of the garden such as a clump of trees or a church spire – really any point of interest. Take care, however, to disguise unwanted focal points like a neighbour's shed or adjacent road signs. There is also a danger that too many such focal points will vie for your attention. Children's play equipment can be a problem here as it tends to be brightly coloured, so look for swings and slides in natural materials with muted colours or possibly use screening to keep play areas hidden.

Some gardens are blessed with wonderful panoramic views of distant hills or seascapes, and if you are in that lucky position then try framing the view with trees or other planting. The effect is often more dramatic than seeing the whole picture at once. The downside of a view like this is that the garden may be exposed to strong winds, requiring a shelter-belt of planting to allow the garden to be enjoyed in relative comfort. In this instance, you could plan the planting so that it both frames the view and offers a degree of protection.

For most of us the views are within the garden and usually from house windows, so take care when siting washing lines, sheds and swings that they are not in a direct line of vision. The forgotten view is always the one back towards the house which is often the most attractive. Positioning a small seating area or just a simple bench away from the house will draw you out, encouraging movement around the garden and making better use of the overall space.

SOLVING SPACE PROBLEMS

In small family gardens it is essential to make the best possible use of available space and to avoid the clutter created by a plethora of play equipment. Here, you could save space by choosing multipurpose equipment that combines a swing, slide and climbing frame rather than having three separate items. If you just have room for a swing then you could build one with two sturdy timber posts, which would be more compact than the conventional 'A'-frame swing. Ground-level sandpits are a neat idea for small gardens as they can be covered over when not in use with a simple timber lid that finishes flush with surrounding paving. This allows children to pedal their tricycles around over the top of the sandpit, or you may use the space for a table and chairs.

Raised timber decks are very popular and are particularly useful for creating a

level surface over awkward sloping ground. They can also be used to conceal the storage of toys, garden furniture or tools underneath. Garden seats may be folded or stacked when they are not in use to save room, but you could also consider built-in seats against garden walls or raised beds to make the most of vertical surfaces. Low-level barbecues can be covered with a paving slab or panels of slatted timber when not in use to form a low bench. The feature can be extended to incorporate storage cupboards for both barbecue and garden equipment.

Space can be maximised by making good use of the vertical surfaces in the garden. If you would like to introduce a small water feature, then a self-contained wall-mounted fountain would be the best solution as it would need no maintenance, no floor space and would be out of the reach of small children. You do not need wide flowerbeds, either, to benefit from year-round interest from plants. Climbers can be grown up walls and pergolas, providing additional shade. If the pergola extends over the lawn then it could also be used as the frame for a swing.

Saving space

The demand for space in a small garden is high, so where possible try to create structures that fulfil more than one function.

*

Make use of every available vertical surface upon which to grow plants to save on valuable floor space. Plants can be grown against the house and boundary walls and on pergolas to provide an overhead canopy of foliage.

*

Games equipment will take up a lot of room when in use and when in storage so save space where possible. Instead of a free-standing basketball net fit one to a house wall, or if you are lucky enough to have a boundary wall then you can also save room by painting on a goal for football.

LEFT: Small spaces require simple, strong compositions to be truly effective. The timber bench set on to brick paving looks just right against the tall planting. The painted urn completes the picture by complementing the colours of the flowers and trellis.

BELOW: This covered archway is reminiscent of an original arbour or tree tunnel. Light filters through the climbing plants to highlight the bench and table below, where the shape of the arch is echoed in the outline of the bench.

ABOVE: A hidden corner can be a real bonus, as in this garden where the main path leads past a recessed seating area. Almost hidden from view, the blue seats nestle in a shaded recess framed by clipped hedges and flowering shrubs, away from the busier parts of the garden.

RIGHT: It would be hard to resist following the stepping stone path from the honeysuckle archway to the swing.

STRUCTURE AND SERVICES

Once the planning stage has been completed then you can start to look in detail at the structure and components of the garden. Walls, paving and pathways are the expensive part of the budget so you need to get them right first time. Choose materials that will withstand the weather and constant use, at the same time blending in with the house walls and other features in the garden. These structural elements, known as the hard landscaping, should be built to last so it would be a false economy to try to cut corners. Unless you are proficient in brick and stonework you may well want to call in professional landscape contractors to ensure that the structure of the garden will last for many years to come.

ENCLOSURE AND DIVISION

The priority in a family garden with young children is to ensure that the boundaries are enclosed with secure fencing or walls. Construct fences with vertical slats as they are much harder to climb than those with horizontal rails, and they will keep children in as well as intruders out. For peace of mind, keep gates locked when toddlers are playing in the garden and ensure that the locks are fitted beyond a child's reach.

Perimeter walls can form a good visual link with the house but can also be expensive to construct. Remember that depth of planting to obscure the boundary is more important than seeing a line of expensive

walling. It may be preferable to build only a short section of wall to unify the house and garden, then complete the enclosure with planting in front of a cheaper fence. If this section of wall is not right next to the house it could also be used as a practice wall for football and other ball games. Walls constructed from the same material as the house can also be introduced as divisions between different parts of the garden. Dividing screens do not have to be hidden by shrub planting, in fact they can be quite eye-catching features in painted trellis or slatted timber. Hedges may also be used to divide up the garden effectively but avoid barriers of prickly holly, thorny berberis and pyracantha which are not at all child or football friendly.

SURFACES AND PATHWAYS

Hard, paved surfaces are essential close to the house, forming a firm area on which to stand tables and chairs and preventing the transfer of mud from the garden into the house. Concrete paving slabs with a slightly textured finish form an ideal non-slip surface. Small areas of brick paving are fine but can look excessive when laid in large areas, especially next to a brick-built house. In this case, it would look better if stone or concrete slabs were laid with a brick trim or occasional brick insets to provide a visual link with the house. Well-treated softwood or hardwood decks can

LEFT: Unity of strong colours makes this an exciting and vibrant part of the garden. Bright blue links the fence, play equipment and window frames all contrasting well with the yellow ornamental grasses and Robinia tree.

form a wonderful warm surface underfoot for sunny areas, but do keep them clean to prevent the growth of algae and the resulting slippery surface. Shingle can also form a good cheap surface but consider it carefully. It is not ideal for children as it is almost impossible to ride a tricycle on it, it attracts unwelcome visits from cats and it tends to get kicked all over the lawn.

An area of grass is the most sensible surface for games and picnics, providing a foil for surrounding plants in all but the smallest courtyard gardens. Choose a cultivated turf for your lawn which includes a dwarf rye grass, as this is relatively slow growing and will withstand at least some of the wear-and-tear of family games. Allow

LEFT: Panels of reed fencing have been used to form a natural and relatively inexpensive enclosure; the shrub planting at intervals along the fence line makes this boundary even more interesting.

ABOVE: Dividing screens can be eye-catching features as shown in this children's garden where wild animals, which have been painted on to block walls, combine with luxurious foliage in a jungle theme. The whole garden captures the spirit of adventure and fun associated with children's play.

ABOVE LEFT: Bark paths, softened by planting, look particularly good in a woodland setting where they may form a link with play areas surfaced in the same material; bark chips laid over a base of compacted hardcore will prevent pathways becoming too muddy.

ABOVE RIGHT: Pathways should not meander aimlessly but should instead lead you somewhere. This stone path bordered by low clipped hedges has a clear direction towards a seat with a view before turning towards other areas in the garden.

ABOVE: Sleepers and gravel extend into areas of adjacent planting to form a path that is well integrated with its surroundings. This type of pathway encourages a leisurely stroll while enjoying the fragrance released by treading on plants such as thyme set between the sleepers.

the grass to grow longer as you move away from the house, fading into more natural planting at the boundaries. Similarly, longer grass under play equipment means less maintenance and a softer landing. Lawn areas should be kept simple, avoiding tight mowing corners and fiddly narrow paths that are hard to maintain and soon turn to mud. Ensure that lawns finish flush with

paved surfaces and where possible introduce a brick trim to make mowing easy and to avoid time-consuming edge cutting.

Bark chips can also be used under play equipment and they look particularly good in a woodland setting, where the same material can be used to surface pathways. Look for 'play grade' quality bark as other bark is coarser and may splinter. Commercial, rubber safety matting could also be used but it is expensive and is usually produced in very bright colours.

Pathways need to provide access around the whole garden and if they are used regularly they should be constructed to form a firm, hardwearing surface. Small paving units like bricks are ideal as they form a good visual link with other areas of brickwork as well as the house. Make sure that the bricks are suitable for laying as paving and are of the hard, well-fired type.

Gently ramped paths of up to 1:10 can be constructed to avoid building steps that are awkward for children, lawn mowers and wheelbarrows. Generous path widths of 90cm (3ft) allow you to walk comfortably even with plants tumbling over the edge. For two people to walk side by side you would need to allow for a width of 120cm (4ft) and this would probably only be suitable in a fairly large garden. Fragrant herbs are pleasant to brush past at the side of a path but steer clear of prickly bushes and irritants such as euphorbia.

SERVICES

Installing electricity can be a real bonus in a garden but the work should be done by a qualified electrician. Electricity is a hidden danger so do pay for the job to be carried out properly. An electrician can prepare a

would otherwise be a wasted dark space. Lighting should be planned to combine both function and aesthetics, illuminating a flight of steps or accentuating the form of a graceful tree. A combination of these two forms of lighting will also provide a degree of security in a far more subtle way than the ubiquitous and far from subtle floodlight. Low-voltage lighting is probably best for garden use unless you have a feature such as a large tree, which may be better lit by more powerful uplighting. Low voltage is safer to use and the light fittings tend to be small which makes them easy to set among low-level planting.

cable plan for you, showing the planned circuit around the garden with various positions indicated for electric sockets to run power tools and pumps for water features. Power can also be run to sheds and greenhouses as well as to several lights around the garden. Where possible, plan for the cables to run alongside boundaries out of harm's way and try to avoid areas of regular cultivation, even though the cable should be buried about 60cm (2ft) below the ground. Armoured cable is recommended for supplying electricity in the garden and it should always be wired back into a circuit breaker to switch off the power instantly if the cable is cut through.

Lighting will extend your use of the garden after dusk, bringing to life what

ABOVE LEFT: Mown grass paths through rough cut meadows or orchards can be extremely effective and one of the simplest types of path to create. They are also easy to grow out and mow in a new position for a complete change of direction.

ABOVE RIGHT: Well positioned planting prevents a short cut straight to the covered sitting area and encourages a walk along the staggered sett path. A weak mortar mix brushed into the joints between the setts will allow mosses to grow and soften the stone.

There is no doubt that the best approach to planting is to grow plants best suited to the particular conditions of your plot rather than persevering, for example, with sun- and moisture-loving plants in dry shade. Having said that, even the right choice of plants will need a little help, especially in the first two seasons after planting, and a simple form of irrigation that dribbles water to the base of the plants will help them to establish in their early years. There is no need for fancy pop-up sprinklers; instead, a very low-tech form of perforated pipe can be trailed around your shrub beds and covered with mulch. A timer to control irrigation can be fitted to an outside tap and set to come on, perhaps twice a day, in the same manner as your central heating. This will enable you to water your plants even when you are away on holiday, ensuring good plant establishment and avoiding expensive losses.

AVOIDING HAZARDS

Safety is of paramount importance in a family garden, both for youngsters who are unaware of the dangers and the elderly who may be unsteady on their feet. Thought must be given to safety during the planning and construction stages as well as in the regular maintenance of the garden. Paved surfaces should be well laid and should, ideally, have a textured surface to help grip. Particular care is needed in the planning and construction of steps, which should also be correctly proportioned and structurally sound. A tried and tested rule of thumb for step proportions is for the sum of the tread width, plus twice the height of the riser, to equal 65cm (26in). These proportions allow a comfortable ascent

ABOVE: A terrace of solid paving leads out on to a lawn where the same paving has been laid with open grass joints. The path changes further to stepping stones in the lawn completing the progression from a frequently used terrace through to an informal sitting area.

Irrigation is also well worth considering when planning your new garden. A simple outside tap may well be sufficient in a small garden where your only real concern is the watering of potted plants. In a larger plot, which perhaps includes a vegetable garden, you may want to run a mains supply out to a tap in the garden to save you dragging a hose all the way from the house, which results in a drop in water pressure.

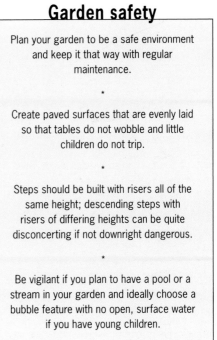
and descent without fear of losing your footing. Steps should also be kept in good order, repairing any loose slabs or bricks before an accident occurs.

All timber work should be well treated and kept in sound condition to avoid both rot and splinters. Particular attention must be paid to fences to make sure that there are no loose slats through which youngsters can escape. Other people's cats can be a real pest in the garden and can be a serious problem for children, so do ensure that sandpits have lids and remember to put them back on to the pits when the children have finished playing.

Water is an obvious hazard in the garden, so until children are old enough to be aware of the danger you would be wise to stick to safe water features. Water bubbling up through a millstone, rocks or pebbles can be very appealing and has no surface water to cause problems. Paddling pools are a source of endless fun but toddlers playing in them need to be supervised all the time.

It goes without saying that great care must be taken when storing garden tools, machinery and chemicals. Ideally, they should be kept under lock and key or at least out of the reach of children. Bottles of weedkiller and fertiliser can look appealing so it is imperative that they are not only stored on high, inaccessible shelves but that they are never decanted into old lemonade bottles or other familiar containers. If you do use power tools in your garden then it would be wise to wait until young children are indoors or under supervision away from where you are working, as these tools can be extremely noisy making it impossible to hear children wandering close to the danger zone. Electric cables should not be used when anyone is playing in the garden. If you do use an electric mower or other electrical tools, wait until everyone is out of the way and, for your own safety, do fit a circuit breaker which will automatically cut off the power should the cable become damaged.

ABOVE: Orchard areas make perfect playgrounds with trees to climb, swings over soft grass and mown paths to chase around. Low maintenance has introduced an element of humour here as the untrimmed grass around the base of the tree trunks resembles fluffy tiger feet.

LEFT: The warm terracotta brick path leads the eye straight towards the focal point of a sundial. However, the watering cans, camouflaged by the heavy planting, could trip up someone as they make their way towards the sundial. Try to keep paths clear from obstacles.

PLANTING FOR PEOPLE

Family life can be extremely hectic and time consuming with parents working, school runs, junior sports teams to watch at weekends, clubs and holidays all leaving very little time for gardening. Low maintenance should, therefore, be one of your top priorities when planning a new garden so that the free time you do have can be spent relaxing or playing rather than staking, tying and pruning. Many people seem to spend hours each week looking after gardens that they are dissatisfied with. This must be a real chore. What you should be doing is spending a short time maintaining a garden that gives you real pleasure. The secret, then, is to create a low-maintenance garden that is right for you whether you are starting from scratch or making alterations to an existing plot.

LAWNS

Choosing grass as a ground cover is the foremost consideration in a family garden and can also reduce the amount of work in the garden. If you have just moved into a new house and the builders have left you no more than a sea of mud outside the back door then you will need to lay a lawn, preferably by turfing rather than by sowing seed. Turfing is the more expensive option but you will obviously be able to use the lawn far more quickly than if you wait for seeds to grow, and the finished result is usually more satisfactory overall.

Lawns that are laid with tough hard-wearing grass need little mowing if they are in constant use, unless you want a bowling green finish which will require a little additional care. Grass mixes today will often contain dwarf rye grasses, which are tough and do not need constant mowing. In fact, grass is best left slightly longer as it is softer to walk on, is not scalped by mowers where the ground is uneven and will not scorch and weaken in hot weather. It also looks better to let grass grow longer at the far end of the lawn as it gives the impression of disappearing into a more natural environment. Taking close-mown grass right up to the boundaries looks artificial and tends to make the plot seem smaller by highlighting the perimeter of the garden. Grass needs to be left longer in more woodland areas to enable it to flourish in the lower light levels. Pathways can also be mown through the long grass to lead you to a gateway, seat or pond – a technique that looks really effective.

Maintenance should always be kept to a minimum if you want to enjoy your garden rather than work in it, so try cutting your grass without collecting the cuttings. If you cut the grass regularly the cuttings will be returned to the lawn as a fine powder, adding valuable nutrients which will save you both the job of feeding the lawn and raking up grass cuttings. Keep lawns to simple, smooth lines and easy shapes to

ABOVE: A good hard-wearing lawn is an essential ingredient in a family garden, offering both somewhere to sit and to play. In this garden the border has been extended into the lawn to create movement, while the change in level up to the bench provides additional interest.

mow, bringing edges of paving flush with the lawn so that you can mow straight over them without the need for trimming the edges. There is no need either for little concrete upstands around a lawn nor gullies next to brick walls; both are unnecessary and require additional work in trimming up. If you do have an edging between lawn and shrub borders then set it flush with the lawn, so that you can mow over the top of it without trimming. Where lawn comes up against a wall you do need a mowing edge but here you can simply lay a line of bricks or paving slabs next to the wall, flush with the lawn, again to avoid laborious trimming.

Sowing grass seed is a cheaper operation taking far longer to produce a usable lawn and if germination is poor the resulting surface can be unsatisfactory. When a new lawn is sown it is inevitable that annual weed seeds will germinate before the grass and although these weeds will mow out in time most people, despite being forewarned, are quite disappointed. It is for these reasons that I recommend that the main lawn be laid to turf so that, sooner rather than later, the family have somewhere attractive to sit out and play. For areas of grass that are on the periphery of the lawn, perhaps to be left longer, I would recommend that these be sown with grass seed, which is the cheaper option, and many of these areas are quite large and the need for quick establishment is not so pressing.

LEFT: Catching a glimpse of a garden beyond an open gate is always intriguing; here the stepping stones help to draw you through to the garden beyond as well as serving a purely practical function in preventing the narrow grass track becoming worn and muddy.

ABOVE: Large grey slab stepping stones, which have been laid through the lawn and run parallel to the beech hedge, provide a strong sense of direction and focus attention on the gate leading into the sunny part of the garden which lies beyond the tree.

Grass is not the only plant that can be used for a lawn – low creeping herbs such as thyme and chamomile can be grown to form fragrant carpets, but their use will be limited as it is only grass that will stand up to constant wear.

USEFUL AND HAZARDOUS PLANTS

Choose plants that are right for the conditions in your garden as this will save you a lot of trouble in the long run. Although you may like azaleas you will be wasting your time trying to grow them if the soil in your garden has a very high chalk content. Do not try to fight nature, but rather work with it by choosing the most suitable plants.

Pulling weeds from around plants is always a time-consuming exercise and can be avoided if plants are planned to grow in bold drifts, covering the ground completely. This sort of planting also provides the garden with a structure, mainly in the form of shrubs, evergreen perennials and ornamental grasses, a combination that results in a stylish planting scheme that requires attention perhaps only once a year.

Avoid gaudy, annual bedding schemes that are costly to install, need regular watering and leave the ground bare of plants for much of the year. These delicate planting schemes are not terribly practical in a family garden. Large gardens with numerous zones may have the luxury of including a special area of such planting, but smaller family gardens do not and must rely on fairly tough shrubs to stand up to games of hide and seek and a variety of vigorous football games. In a small garden, the show of

ABOVE: Herbs not only provide fragrance but flavouring for cooking, too, and, like this low-growing thyme, they are also quick and easy to establish.

RIGHT: Fruit and vegetable plots need not be dull areas banished to the end of the garden but rather they can be colourful, vibrant places full of interest. They can also be places in which to spark a child's interest in gardening and an awareness of the environment. Maintaining interest will be helped by sowing colourful and easy to grow plants such as wigwams of runner beans or drifts of nasturtiums for a riot of late summer colour.

colour produced by this type of planting is probably best limited to containers where the effect is less dramatic, both on the eye and the pocket.

Using a greenhouse to its full potential in a low-maintenance garden is a contradiction in terms, so unless you are very keen and have plenty of time it is probably wise to leave the idea well alone. Growing fruit and vegetables, however, can be good fun and is extremely rewarding despite the level of maintenance needed for their cultivation. It is possible to take certain steps to reduce the amount of work involved. Plants grown in small, deep, raised beds are easy to care for and a simple irrigation system will save on manual watering, while a layer of mulch will help to retain moisture and prevent weeds germinating.

If you do not have the room, or the time, for a separate vegetable garden you can always integrate a small amount of fruit and vegetables with your other plants. Radishes, strawberries and carrots are all quick and easy to grow, and a wigwam of runner beans takes up very little room and looks stunning when in flower. Small fruit trees fit into a modest garden but they will still need training and spraying and will also attract unwelcome wasps in the summer.

Herbs are also a useful addition to garden planting. A wide variety of herbs can be grown quite easily and cheaply and they lend the garden a wonderful fragrance and colour, as well as providing a fresh home-grown source of flavouring for cooking. Many herbs such as sage, chives, rosemary and oregano are simple to grow, requiring only a sunny spot and well-drained soil, while some herbs like thyme can be established in the joints between paving stones.

There are many plants that would not do you a lot of good if you ate them, but there are some such as daphne, laburnum and yew that are far more poisonous than others. Some plants do not even have to be ingested to cause a problem: euphorbia and several conifer varieties can irritate the skin if you simply come into contact with the foliage. Certain other plants present a hazard simply by the nature of their vicious thorns or spiny leaves.

There are plenty of plants to choose for your garden without selecting any of those on the danger list, but if you have a particular favourite that you feel you really must include then make sure that you plant it well away from play areas and swimming pools. It may also be wise to avoid planting the real villains until your children are old enough to understand the dangers and to resist their curiosity.

TOP: Some hazardous plants can poison or irritate while others are just plain vicious; this agave has had its sharply pointed, sword-like leaves capped with corks to prevent injury to those who step too close.

ABOVE: A mound of golden thyme in a stone pot becomes a simple focal point in this herb garden, while a collection of grasses surrounding it add movement and changing colours throughout the year.

have eye-catching results – nasturtiums, sunflowers and sweetpeas are all good choices. Consider too fruit and vegetables that are both easy to grow and appealing to eat – carrots and radishes for example.

As children grow up and work with you in the garden you can begin to make them aware of the hazards of certain plants and to teach them about the safe handling of tools and equipment. Try not to make it all too dull, though, as some jobs like raking leaves can be more fun with children even if it does take a lot longer.

THE GROWING GARDEN

As the family grows up and requirements change, the garden can be adapted to those different needs. A water feature may start as a safe dry stream, possibly with a bubbling water fountain through rocks and pebbles, but when children are older, the stones may be removed to form a beach and the stream filled with running water.

The key to a changeable feature such as this is good planning, ensuring that the stream is excavated to the correct depth initially to avoid too much disruption later on. Similarly, sandpits set in patio areas can, at a later stage, be converted into pools by lining them with a butyl rubber liner and relaying a brick edge coping to finish flush with the paving. A swing secured to a sturdy pergola can be removed when no longer needed without changing the garden design.

When children are very young you may feel better if they play close by you under your careful supervision. However, slightly older children enjoy some seclusion – maybe a sandpit half hidden by planting but still within the earshot of parents. As children grow older, and if space allows,

ENCOURAGING CHILDREN IN THE GARDEN

Young children like to help with jobs in the garden so make the most of it before they grow up. Try to encourage them to become involved in a variety of jobs, which also include growing plants rather than just the weeding. The simple process of sowing seeds in a container or planting bulbs in a small patch of ground will create an interest in the environment and an awareness of the changing seasons. It will help if you choose plants that are fairly quick to respond and

they may wish to venture further, safe within the confines of their own garden but free from the watchful eyes of adults. A graduation of different playing zones can be created using simple screens of hedges and shrubs, making subtle divisions between areas moving further away from the house. Planning a garden for the future and not just the short term will mean a smooth transition from one stage to the next without either expensive disruption or obsolete garden features.

Planting for families

Choose tough plants like viburnum, nandina and cistus to provide structure and interest throughout the year. Bamboo is another useful plant as it is a tough evergreen but also extremely graceful.

*

Ground cover plants can be used to form a green carpet and to keep down weeds. Plants such as bergenia and *Liriope muscari* are ideal as they are both evergreen and will provide interest all year round.

*

Avoid poisonous plants like laburnum, yew and daphne until your children are old enough to understand the potential dangers of such plants. Prickly plants such as berberis, pyracantha and holly are also best avoided.

*

Try to encourage children in the garden. Projects like planting easy to grow flowers such as nasturtiums and sunflowers will bring quick and satisfying results.

ABOVE: Tall grasses provide a relaxed atmosphere within a garden and are great fun for children to play hide-and-seek in.

RIGHT: In this garden, a neat combination of poles and climbing bars could change its use to a support on which to train plants when the children grow older and their play has moved further away from the house.

relaxation

RELAXATION

Making time to relax in the garden should be a

RIGHT: Escaping to a quiet corner of your garden is for many people the perfect way in which to relax. This secluded position is an ideal retreat in the light shade of adjacent trees with walls and fences covered in cool green foliage. The lounger can easily be wheeled to another position, perhaps for a snooze.

Gardens form an escape route from the busy world of families and work, providing a calm space for relaxation. Today everything runs on such a tight schedule whether it is work, mealtimes, school runs, clubs or holidays that we need to make sure that somewhere in there we can also find time for ourselves. Nearly everyone needs to make a conscious effort to switch off and most people look for that peace and quiet in the natural world. While working days can fly by with never enough time to do it all, a walk in the country without the pressure of time can seem to last forever.

OPPOSITE: For true relaxation it is important to find a place away from the house and play areas. Here, a lightweight chair has been taken to such a place in the depths of the garden: a small stone terrace with light filtering through the branches of the tree canopy overhead and with views over the surrounding garden.

LEFT: This beautifully designed and totally private garden retreat is ideal for relaxation with a hammock for sleeping in the sun and a slatted bench with cushions for relaxing in the shade. Decorated in cool white with climbing plants trailing through the rafters, the timber shelter allows you to relax here even during summer showers.

priority for everyone.

The same timeless quality that is found in the natural world can be found in the sanctuary of your garden. Relaxing in the garden can give you time to unwind and clear your mind. Even children as they grow older will begin to look for their own space in order to get away from younger brothers and sisters, the pressures of homework, and even their parents.

One of the ways in which the relaxing influence of the natural world can be brought into the garden is by introducing water into your design. Water can be extremely therapeutic and may be incorporated as a small fountain or bubble feature. On the other hand, if you have more land, a large part of your plot could be developed as a water garden full of reflections and leafy waterside walks. Using fragrant plants or those that rustle gently in a breeze can enhance your relaxation area. You may even wish to plan a Zen-style area into a small corner of the garden for meditation and true spiritual refreshment. A maze of beech or hornbeam hedges could perhaps form the most intriguing way of reaching your relaxation garden, for there cannot be a better way in which to create a secret hideaway than by making a puzzle for people to solve in order to reach it.

It is a good idea to allocate a specific area of the garden for relaxation. Plan it away from the house and play areas so you can be assured of peace and quiet. You will be able to relax far more easily if you are in a serene, secluded space so create a screen of shrubs, trellis or bamboo to hide the washing and the neighbours. Noise, especially traffic, can be an intrusion over which you have no control and which you cannot hope to block out entirely. You can, however, introduce a 'masking' sound – the rustling leaves of bamboo or the sound of a bubbling fountain – that will help to tone down the background noise. Even in the heart of the city, a small courtyard garden can be softened by planting, while overhead beams or small trees will hide you from view so that you can, if you wish, forget your urban location.

Finally, your choice of planting will go a long way to creating the right atmosphere in your garden. Fragrant plants in cool greens and whites are relaxing and easy on the eye. Avoid too many vibrant, clashing colours that may ultimately prove over stimulating and stressful.

ESCAPING

The easiest way to escape is to find a quiet corner to sit in and let the world drift by. That place might be a seat under a tree with the light filtering through branches or a cosy hideaway surrounded by all your favourite books. Tree seats are inviting and there is a greater feeling of comfort and security when sitting with your back protected by a large tree as opposed to sitting out in the middle of the lawn. You may find it best to choose a place hidden from neighbours who may wish to chat, and a place with some privacy if you want to sunbathe.

'Escape' will mean different things to different people. In its simplest form it can mean sitting undisturbed in a quiet corner of your garden, perhaps watching a gentle running stream or the ripples formed by dropping pebbles into a still pool. A secret garden may be planned in a sheltered corner as an inner sanctuary to shut out the world or you could include an arbour in which to sit in a cool and shaded spot.

You will also need to think about the style of furniture in your garden. Portable garden furniture should be lightweight and

ABOVE: Garlanded with scented roses and apparently held in place by surrounding foliage, this timber bench looks to be the epitome of comfort and relaxation.

LEFT: Timber steps lead down through lush planting to a secluded deck extending out over a pool, where two sleek steamer chairs allow you to while away long and lazy afternoons.

OPPOSITE: In this garden where the sitting area is partly enclosed by the foliage of the small trees and shrubs, sunlight filters through on to piles of cushions, creating an extremely relaxed atmosphere.

comfortable, easy to move as you follow the sun, or shade, around into different positions in the garden. Rattan is lightweight and elegant, reminiscent of a colonial style when set against palms and tropical foliage. Plastic or resin chairs can be stacked or folded for easy carrying and storage, while the classic deckchair is portable and fits in with any style. Elegant French café-style furniture has folding metal legs with lightweight wooden slats for seat and back and is just right for sitting down to enjoy a cup of coffee and a croissant.

SECRET GARDENS

Hidden gardens have been designed for peace and tranquillity throughout the centuries, from the cool retreat of traditional Islamic gardens to the peaceful meditation spaces of Buddhist priests. In medieval times Christianity also developed this style of inner sanctuary in the cloistered gardens of large abbeys and cathedrals.

The inclusion of a hidden retreat within a garden adds a special atmosphere and a sense of intrigue. But to be truly relaxing it should be sited away from play equipment and family areas, and shrubs or hedges can be planted to retain the privacy of the space all year round. Beech and hornbeam both have fresh green leaves in the spring which turn brown in the autumn but are held on the branches all winter. Yew could also be planted as it is evergreen, but its

RIGHT: An arbour covered in scented honeysuckle provides a good alternative to a secret garden. Cool, shaded and fragrant, this arbour forms an ideal place in which to sit and enjoy some peace and tranquillity.

BELOW: Cats often find the best place to sit and this one is no exception, having found a perfect place in a chink of sunlight under a vine-covered arbour.

association with churchyards may create a sombre atmosphere. Woodland clearings often provide the most wonderful hidden gardens, and for a truly spiritual retreat you can plant light foliage birch trees that will filter shafts of sunlight into a cool acer glade. It is often best to use light deciduous trees such as birch which allows light to shine through on to autumn colours. Trees with a dark overhead canopy can create a sense of mystery but their shadow may appear cold and uninviting.

Plan your secret garden carefully and simply. There is no need for any great construction but the site should be positioned away from noisy areas and overlooking windows. Paths leading into the hidden garden should be on firm ground, possibly made from bark chippings so that you can escape there even if the surrounding ground is damp underfoot. A far greater sense of mystery can be introduced by making the path appear to vanish before opening out into a small paved space or a grassy woodland clearing. A fountain or a still pool can also be added, but make sure there is sufficient room for seating as well.

ARBOURS

A leafy bower or a rose-scented arbour are good alternatives to a secret garden — shaded by a canopy of fragrant, twining climbers and enclosed on three sides, an arbour is the ideal place to curl up and read a book. Traditional arbours, with their long shaded tunnels, encouraged movement

LEFT: Arbours today have evolved from the long shaded tunnels through which to walk into smaller shaded retreats such as this one, where the white seat acts as a focal point drawing you to it to sit and unwind.

ABOVE: The structure of this arbour has been completely overgrown, creating a dense wall of foliage with just a few narrow openings. If there is no opportunity to create a secret woodland garden then this leafy bower is a great idea.

within the garden. They also lent mystery and intrigue, but were not designed primarily as areas for relaxation. Today's arbours, however, have evolved into smaller, shaded retreats in which to sit and unwind. They are often positioned as focal points, attracting the eye and drawing you out into the garden, or they may be sited to the side of long walkways. In these positions they are fine for a short rest or as a comfortable place from which to oversee children's games, but for true relaxation the arbour needs to be hidden – a secret and special place out of the view of the house and away from children and chatty neighbours.

Arbours should be simple to construct: a sturdy post in each of the four corners joined at the top with overhead beams to support evenly spaced rafters. The back and two sides may be filled in with trellis or slatted timber and you could also build in a timber bench or simply bring a portable seat with you. It is possible to buy arbours in kit form in timber or thin sections of black tubular steel. These constructions are easy to fit together, although some of them are a bit flimsy and will probably not support the weight of heavy climbers like wisteria. If you have a wall against which your arbour can be positioned then this will provide a strong support for the overhead beams. In a woodland setting you may be tempted by the rural charm of an arbour made from rustic poles – but do not succumb as the poles will soon deteriorate and the structure will be short-lived.

RIGHT: Planting around an arbour or setting it back into mature shrubs will help to blend the structure into the garden. This particular arbour will soon be clothed in foliage to leave only a framed view out on to the sunlit garden.

OPPOSITE: A hut in the garden can provide the perfect escape for adults or children; a place for model making or a hideaway which could easily be a studio for painting or potting.

Choose a style of arbour that is suitable for your garden and is right for you. In general, traditional arbours in wrought iron or hardwood may be best suited to the country garden of a period house rather than a more streamlined or contemporary property – but it is really a matter of choice. A mix of styles can be successful especially in the space offered by a large garden but, ultimately, the aim is to clothe the arbour in foliage, making its construction material a matter of secondary importance.

Planting around the arbour will help to create privacy and foster a feeling of seclusion. This can be achieved easily by setting the structure back into existing mature shrubs. Hedging plants such as hornbeam can be trained to grow around and through the arbour to form a green surround, and the addition of two or three small trees will provide a canopy of overhanging branches. Climbers may also be planted to twine around overhead beams. They give quick cover and are often beautifully fragrant. Honeysuckle is a scented woodland climber and is, therefore, particularly suitable while varieties like the evergreen *Lonicera japonica* 'Halliana' will provide a covering of foliage all year. In woodland areas *Clematis montana* and the scented *C. armandii* will tolerate the lower light levels of dappled shade. And for a secluded rose-scented arbour you could try *Rosa* 'Madame Alfred Carrière', a pale pink rose that will tolerate more shady conditions than many other roses. All you need now are the comforts of a folding chair and table and maybe a lantern to lead you to your hidden retreat.

HUTS AND HIDEAWAYS

There is something magical about the phrase 'huts and hideaways' that conjures up a picture far more enchanting than 'sheds'. Sheds imply work – lawn mowers and compost, seed trays and spray – while huts can be whatever you want them to be, a wonderful place of escape for children and adults alike no matter what the weather. A hut can be where you indulge in your hobby, perhaps making models, or it may be that you want a hideaway as a studio for painting or potting. It may look small and insignificant from the outside but can open up into

LEFT: A hut may look small and insignificant from the outside but inside it may open up into a magical and beautifully furnished little room in which to relax.

ABOVE: Almost hidden from view, this hut or children's den nestles among dense planting at the end of the garden, where it enjoys more seclusion than most with the use of a ladder to gain access to the secret hideaway.

a different world inside – similar to the beach huts lined up on the front at an English seaside resort, which open up to reveal a room furnished with small tables and chairs, storage cupboards and book shelves, folding beds and towel racks.

While the open structure of an arbour requires a secluded position to maintain privacy, a hut can be positioned in a more open space as doors, shutters and maybe curtains will hide you from the outside world. However, a hut must still sit comfortably in the garden, perhaps half hidden by plants or nestling back against mature shrubs. The style and material of the construction are also important, whether it is a ready-to-assemble sectional building or your own design. Have a look at those on display in a garden centre and adapt the design, altering the shape and size to suit your own garden. Stain or paint the building in keeping with your chosen style. This could be in bright colours for a Mediterranean feel or in more muted colours to blend in with the planting of a country garden. Painting the inside of the building will brighten it up and make the space seem bigger and more airy and you could even introduce some simple

OPPOSITE: This white-painted veranda is a wonderful space to sit and relax in the open air with the protection of a roof to afford shelter from unwelcome showers.

LEFT: A summerhouse will often be positioned to command a good view over the garden which can be enjoyed with afternoon tea or an evening drink as the sun sets.

LEFT: Be sure when buying a summerhouse such as this, that it will remain as a relaxing retreat and not degenerate into a glorified storage shed.

stencilled patterns on the walls. For a real hideaway, add chairs, a small sofa and table and, if possible, run electricity out from the house for lights and music. Otherwise a gas lantern and a portable CD player will do just as well.

A children's hut could be themed, but do not be tempted to overdo it for as the children grow older you may find that your streetwise eleven-year-old is not too impressed with the Postman Pat scene you painted for him when he was only two. Keep it simple, maybe with a hint of a nautical or seaside theme – model boats on the shelves, shells and pictures of the sea. Furnishings can be simple too with rush mats or rugs, big cushions, a small table and stools all combining to make the perfect den. Also, as the children grow up their hideaway becomes just that, so decorations that can easily be changed or painted over are a good idea, too.

Treehouses are the ultimate hideaway for both children and adults but they must be soundly built in a strong tree and reached by a sturdy ladder. They can be a wonderful place to escape to, full of adventure with rope swings and lookout places where the children can play or you can retreat to in order to do some reading or writing away from the noise of family life.

SUMMERHOUSES, PAVILIONS AND GAZEBOS

These buildings, which may be positioned to form eye-catching focal points or set to command wonderful views of the surrounding countryside, convey an altogether grander image than any hideaway. Such buildings are for the pleasurable relaxation of afternoon tea or an evening drink while watching the setting sun. They are built for comfort and shelter, often with scented planting around them to create a very special atmosphere. So think very carefully before buying one. You must be sure that you want somewhere for relaxation and not storage. Expensive summerhouses are so often bought and set in a prime position within the garden with the lawnmower, boxes and racks of children's bikes clearly visible through their windows. Don't spoil the effect – use the garage for storage or a shed hidden out of the way.

If you do indulge in the luxury of a summerhouse then take care to site it so that it draws you out into the garden,

RIGHT: Positioned as a focal point and from which to enjoy wonderful views, this white gazebo looks stunning set among the autumn colours.

BELOW: Gazebos are usually designed so that you can enjoy glorious views. This is a prime example, where the gazebo forms a wonderful resting place to enjoy the view and retreat into welcome shade.

OPPOSITE: The outline of the large parasol links perfectly with the roofline of the summerhouse that has been set in a commanding position over the pool in which it is reflected.

Swiss chalet or log cabin. Some buildings at the top end of the market are pure luxury, often built from fine hardwood with brass fittings, fully lined and insulated – in fact so warm and dry that you could move in and live there.

Gazebos, on the other hand, are open-sided buildings designed for open settings from which to enjoy panoramic views. They are often set into a garden as a focal point and may be painted in bright colours, but they should not be hidden in foliage as the whole point of the open sides is for viewing. Gazebos provide a place to sit in peace and quiet from which to enjoy views over your garden and ideally over the surrounding fields or crashing surf, for the ultimate in relaxation and escapism.

framing it with shrub planting and softening the roofline with overhanging branches. A firm path should be constructed to give you access from the house or terrace, and the structure should not be positioned too far away; you do not want to walk forever to get there and if it is hidden from sight you may never use it at all. Occasional low lights along the path will lead the way, with additional lighting in the summerhouse to provide a warm glow by which to read or enjoy that quiet drink.

Pavilions imply a far larger summerhouse with double doors and a veranda, really only suitable for a large garden. Inside there should be room for a table, several chairs and a couch to provide a very grand garden room in which to relax. Summerhouses and pavilions are available as sectional buildings, but some of these can be over-the-top, often looking like a

Looking after materials

Galvanised metal features require no maintenance, but anything made of plastic-coated tubular steel – such as arbours and some types of garden furniture – will need to be wiped down occasionally. Untreated metal features should be painted with a modern paint containing a rust inhibitor.

*

Softwood timber furniture, buildings and wooden arbours should be pressure treated before construction and regularly painted with preservative to avoid rot. Hardwood furniture need not be treated but the occasional application of teak oil will help preserve the original colour.

*

Plastic furniture can be left out in all weathers although it is light enough to move into storage when not in use. To keep plastic looking good, clean with soapy water and a non-scratch cloth.

WATER

ABOVE: A millstone water feature is ideal for a young family garden as the moving water will enthral children for hours. There is also a hidden reservoir covered in pebbles so that there is no open surface of water to cause concern.

Water can certainly enhance the atmosphere of any garden whether it is splashing over mossy rocks in a shady secret garden or as a stone-edged pool surrounded by plants to attract birds. In a natural setting, you can sit forever and watch a babbling brook splashing over pebbles, catching the light in different ways, eddying and swirling after small waterfalls. Still pools and lakes have great reflective qualities and can be used to mirror buildings, trees or simply the sky in a style reminiscent of the hot courtyards of the Spanish Alhambra. Or, if you prefer the illusion of a coastal retreat, you could set your pump on a timer to send the water splashing back and forth across rocks to

recreate the familiar sound of breaking waves. Throughout history water has introduced life and movement into gardens and you are indeed lucky if you live close to the sea or if a stream flows along the bottom of your garden.

All these images can be echoed in your garden where even the smallest plot will have room for some sort of water feature. There may not be space for a lake or mountain torrent but these can be scaled down to a size that is appropriate for your garden. One of the great pleasures of water is its attraction to wildlife. New ponds can be constructed and the very next day, seemingly from nowhere, dragonflies will appear and skit across the surface of the water. When new housing developments are built the natural wildlife disappears, often taking years to come back; planting trees and shrubs will certainly speed up that return as will the introduction of water. Even a birdbath or small splash pool will help to bring new life back into the garden.

Planting at the water's edge and even in the water itself introduces a totally different atmosphere into the garden - that of a river bank. Here, choosing the right plants for the location helps to create the illusion of a riverside setting, with the added advantage that water-associated plants are generally fast growing and so the desired effect is produced very quickly.

LEFT: A large pool or lake associates well with the natural landscape. The pool which has been created here is a perfect example in a wonderful setting with a backdrop of distant mountain peaks. The treatment of the water's edge is, however, the key to a successful design and here tall water-associated plants and beach pebbles all help to conceal the edge, ensuring that the natural appearance of the pool is maintained.

LEFT: Small fountains which bubble up through pebbles should be sited close to the house so the effect can be enjoyed from both inside and out.

RIGHT: An effective water feature need not be too complicated; here, water simply falls from one stone trough to another before overflowing into a sump to be recycled.

ABOVE AND RIGHT: Narrow water channels are linked to a shallow pool in this well designed garden. The channels start as a dish shape which mirrors the outline of the ceramic plates used within the garden. The streams, which are laid out as a cross that cuts the garden into four sections, finish at the shallow rectangular pool. Soft pink flowers reflect both the edging and coping stones as well as the gravel used to surface pathways throughout the garden.

DESIGN AND PRACTICALITIES

Plan your water feature at an early stage as it does involve a great deal of excavating work, the use of heavy machinery and the laying of pipe runs, none of which is best dealt with as an afterthought. Have a careful look at the levels in your garden, for although you may prefer a pond close to your house, if that position is at the top of a slope then it may look decidedly odd as natural ponds would obviously form in hollows. Flat gardens can also prove tricky if you are trying to introduce a natural-looking pool, as any artificial slopes often need to be constructed over a large area of the garden to blend in. Placing a small mound in the corner of a flat garden simply to provide height for a waterfall does not create the illusion of a natural feature and can look quite ridiculous.

Style must also be considered carefully as even in an age of 'anything goes' in the garden, a mountain stream in a city garden may look somewhat incongruous. Scale is important, too, as all areas of the garden should be in proportion. A small pool in a large garden can look lost unless, of course, it has been set in a specific area in the garden. Equally, large pools will dominate a small space allowing no room to soften the water's edge and the boundary fences; it would be far better in this case to show glimpses of a much smaller pool which hint at a larger expanse of hidden water.

Lack of access to the garden can cause real problems and can actually influence your choice of water feature. If you have a closed site with the only access to your garden through the house, then clearly a large pool requiring heavy machinery is out of the question. Cranes can sometimes be used to lift excavating machinery over walls, but you would have to look carefully at the risks involved and whether the expense of such an operation can really be justified.

Safety is the first priority when planning a water feature for a family garden. In these cases, you could choose a bubble feature where water is fed from a hidden reservoir to froth over cobbles or an old millstone without any surface area of water to worry you. This type of feature is best sited close to the house from where it can be clearly seen and enjoyed from both inside and out.

If you would like a stream in your garden and you have young children, it is possible to start out with a dry stone watercourse in the style of a Japanese garden. If you dig the mock 'stream' to the correct depth initially and inset a liner then you could convert it into a real water feature when the children are older without too much disruption to the rest of the garden.

Small still, reflecting pools need only be shallow, but they must be dark-lined for the best reflective quality and to ensure that the bottom of the pool cannot be seen. Setting loose pebbles into a shallow watercourse

ABOVE: Even without adjacent planting, water can be used to good effect in a garden as this simple feature shows; designs such as this tend to work best in an enclosed compact space. Here water emerges through the spout in the back fence to add life and movement, while the raised pool adds relief to this stark landscape.

ABOVE: A simple fountain jet plays into the pool, sending out gentle ripples and splashes; the pool itself is almost hidden from view until you get close and is surrounded by lush planting which helps soften and mask the edge. A seat nearby allows you to sit and relax in this very secret garden.

will create turbulence and spray that will attract small birds. The downside of all shallow water features is that in hot weather the water can evaporate out of the system very quickly. If the pool is small then it may be a simple matter of keeping it topped up by hand. For anything larger you may find it more practical to install an automatic top-up system connected to the mains supply. It is important that the system does not run dry, as this will damage the electric pump.

If you intend to keep fish in your pool it should be at least 60cm (2ft) deep so that the fish have somewhere to escape to if the surface freezes over in winter. Try to avoid

siting the pool underneath trees, as the fallen leaves will rot in the water causing the build-up of a toxin that is harmful to fish. However, a woodland background can look really good, and as it is almost impossible to keep all leaves out of the water you may need to place a net over the surface during the autumn to deal with the problem. Modern butyl rubber liners are the best material from which to construct pools as they can be moulded to fit any shape, they will not crack like concrete should there be any soil movement and their black colour ensures good reflections. It may be wise to plan in a simple overflow pipe in case the water level in your pool rises too high during heavy rainfall and starts to erode the soil in adjacent beds. A pipe set slightly above the desired water level will take any excess water to a ditch or soakaway.

Access to the water's edge is important not only for maintenance and for retrieving footballs but also for your enjoyment and relaxation. Other pathways and waterside walks will always look best in natural materials; bark chippings are best for a natural pathway, and should be laid over a sub-base of compacted hardcore to prevent the path from becoming muddy. Rolled gravel is often laid in larger waterside parks – it is a natural material with a soft colour which compacts to form a hardwearing path. This needs to be watered and compacted with a roller to form a firm surface.

LEFT: Lakes and large pools have superb reflective qualities, here reflecting the trunks of mature trees. This lake is big enough to row a boat across, with a jetty perfect for tying up your boat, sunbathing or simply to sit on while dipping your toes in the cool water.

BELOW: The large pool blends perfectly with the surrounding landscape with the varying shades of green providing a pleasant combination. There is also a good balance of waterlilies and rushes, all of which works well with the shorter grass to the hedge line and the pastures beyond.

FROM FOUNTAINS TO LAKES

There are many small water features which can be used in compact gardens or for specific areas within larger gardens. These systems are very simple, easy to install and, above all, extremely safe. A small tank is set below ground level and acts as a reservoir, above which a section of steel mesh supports a millstone or drilled boulder. A submersible pump set in the reservoir pushes water up through the millstone and over its edge, where it falls back through pebbles into the reservoir. As the tank of water is hidden beneath the surface of the ground safety is not an issue. Wall-mounted features are also safe and easy to install. What is more, they take up very little room, thus making them ideal for small gardens where they will create a point of interest at eye level.

Some wall-mounted fountains are self-contained, spouting a jet of water into a small tank where a pump circulates it. Other fountains spout water into a free-standing tank at ground level or on to loose cobbles that conceal a hidden tank of water containing the submersible pump. There are plenty of interesting features around that you can use as a your fountainhead rather than just settle for the ubiquitous lion's head mask – lizards look particularly good on a hot wall, and a little frog spitting a jet of water from his perch on top of a shiny boulder can look charming.

Pebble-lined splash pools for birds look good but need a position close to the house in order to be viewed from a window. Shallow pools like these can evaporate quite quickly so they will need to be kept topped up to avoid damage to the pump. As with all open pools, care should be taken when young children are around.

In paved areas geometric pools work well when sited close to buildings, where they echo the lines of the house walls. These pools may be raised above ground level to

add vertical interest to a terrace and can also incorporate a built-in bench to provide additional seating. Several pools linked together can be fun, with water cascading from one pool to another. A reflective ground-level pool can look stunning when set close to a building, especially when lit at night. A crisp edging trim to the pool in granite or brick can look really sharp but all this must be set into an area of non-slip paving for obvious safety. Care must also be taken not to site a low-level pool on a direct route out of the house.

ABOVE: Moving water can often bring humour into a garden to make us smile and to help us to relax. This pineapple fountain would certainly cheer you up and make a quirky focal point at the end of the lawn.

LEFT: This is a luxurious setting for a small water garden surrounded by lush planting and bordered by posts. Pots have been used to protect the edge of the pool where the steps come down close to the water.

OPPOSITE: A large formal pool in this Spanish court-yard style garden reflects the buildings and is host to beautiful floating lilies. Paved areas should be wide enough to provide seating areas; on the narrow side of this pool, pots have been positioned to help indicate the edge.

BELOW: A broad timber bridge gives access across this natural pool with its still, reflective qualities in delightful contrast to the arching fountain jet which adds action and movement. The bridge is wide enough to cross in comfort and safety without a handrail.

Larger ponds or even lakes obviously associate well with the natural landscape and are therefore best suited to areas away from the house. If there is room in your garden you could build a watercourse with several pools linked together by streams and small waterfalls, making use of any natural contours so as not to look contrived.

RIGHT: Water often adds the final magical quality to a secret garden for relaxation. Here, a simple bench has been positioned from where to sit and contemplate by the still, dark depths of a pool under the hanging branches of an apple tree.

The treatment of the pond edge is the key to the success or failure of the scheme; a broad band of butyl liner showing above the water level looks awful and instantly removes any illusion of a natural water-course. The best solution is to tuck the liner under the surrounding soil and plant marginals to overhang and soften the water's edge. Timber decking looks perfect next to water and successfully conceals the edge of the pond where it overhangs the surface. Decks make an ideal place to sunbathe or to sit and dabble your toes in the cool water; your deck could even be a jetty to which a

small rowing boat is tied ready for you to row out to the middle of the water for the ultimate getaway.

Water-associated plants carefully positioned, leading away from the pond, will give the illusion of an underground spring or stream. If you extend this planting to your boundary you can create the impression that your pond is truly natural and is fed from a watercourse beyond your garden. Small areas of strewn pebbles are another natural treatment for a pond edge, allowing access for both you and small animals. Lawn rolling down to the water can look wonderful, too, but is best used on larger pools as it tends to act like blotting paper and can quickly cause the water level of a small pool to drop. Lush planting with ligularia, irises, bamboo and other bog-loving plants helps the pond sit comfortably in the landscape.

To create a real bog garden, extend part of the liner out from the pond edge to tuck under a depth of soil. This will ensure that the area is permanently wet, providing the perfect conditions for bog-loving plants. Access through the boggy area can be created using log rounds as stepping stones. Chicken wire stapled to their upper surface will give grip if they become slippery.

Bridges in their various forms can be constructed to give access across a narrow part of the watercourse. Simple designs always look best. A large stone slab or a couple of old railway sleepers would be fine to bridge a narrow stretch of water. Stepping stones require a little more care both with

installation and when crossing the stream. If you have built an area of timber decking adjacent to the water then a bridge in the same material would be in keeping. A handrail to rest against to watch the water flow by is a good idea and perfect for children to lean on when playing games of 'Pooh sticks'.

BELOW: A mown lawn leads down from delicate birch trees to the edge of a pool which separates the cultivated garden from the pastures on the hillside beyond. A raised boardwalk provides access and allows an unhurried walk overlooking the water.

HUMOUR AND OTHER EFFECTS

To smile is to relax and water in its various forms can definitely help both adults and children to achieve this. Children have a particular fascination with moving water and love trying to jump on water jets that spring up intermittently through paved areas or to duck under the flying water fountains in Alice's Curious Labyrinth at Eurodisney. Sculpture and water combine to good effect as in the humorous design of Dennis Fairweather's 'Spouting Water Gargoyle' and the amazing granite kugels where a huge granite sphere is kept spin-

ABOVE: There is really nothing like a hot tub for sheer pleasure and relaxation; ideally the tub should be positioned close to the house or swimming pool with a changing room. Planting and trellis work will give privacy and shelter from cool breezes.

ABOVE RIGHT: It is so much easier to make a pool or a small lake, such as this one, appear natural when it is set against a backdrop of mature trees. The two seats, held in by planting at the water's edge, allow for peaceful conversation.

ning by the power of a water jet. Similarly, water trickling down strained wires will give the illusion of vertical lines of water, while clear plastic half-spheres set into a pool will be reflected as whole spheres or a series of floating bubbles.

Mirrors can also work well with water, set against a wall and masked around the edges with plants to reflect a pool which then seems twice as long. If a bridge is built over the end of a watercourse and concealed to one side with planting, then a mirror set under the bridge will give the illusion that the stream continues on much further.

Hot tubs can also add an extra relaxing dimension to the garden. They should be positioned close to the house or in the vicinity of a swimming pool, with a changing

Hot tubs when full of water and people weigh a tremendous amount so they should always be constructed over a base of reinforced concrete. The surrounding surface should obviously consist of non-slip paving or decking. The same material can also be used to build ledges to sit on and planters for fragrant, softening shrubs. Spiky architectural foliage does associate well aesthetically with decking but should be kept well back from the hot tub, as sharp leaves and bare skin are not a good combination and unpleasant experiences with prickles could spoil your warm water massage.

Care with water features

If you have young children it is best to avoid open water features. You could, however, install a fountain, which bubbles through pebbles, or have a dry stone stream that could be filled with water when the children are older. Self-contained, wall-mounted fountains are an alternative safe water feature that is ideal for small gardens.

*

Pools which are set level with the patio should be sited away from the main access route to the house. Ground-level pools should also be surrounded by non-slip textured paving slabs, brushed concrete or well burnt stock bricks.

*

Submersible pumps for ponds must be plugged into waterproof external sockets. Tall fountains need to be positioned in the centre of a pool to prevent wind blowing the spray away from the pool and thus slowly emptying the whole system of water. In shallow pools, wind-blown spray as well as evaporation can empty the system, causing damage to the submersible pump. It is therefore wise to fit a top-up valve to your pool which will ensure that the water is kept at a constant level and never runs dry.

room, if possible. Shelter from cold wind is essential and here tall plants like grasses and bamboo work well for protection and privacy. I once had clients who enjoyed their hot tub all year long. Before I came along and suggested some screening plants they had been using it totally open to the elements and to view – they were certainly the talk of the neighbourhood.

TOP: Timber has been used for the seats and decking around this hot tub which blends in superbly with its woodland garden setting. Timber could also be used in this setting to build raised planters for fragrant and softening plants.

ABOVE: Tall plants work well with decking and provide both protection and privacy around a hot tub. Any plants which have particularly spiky leaves, however, should be kept back from the water's edge and the bare skin of the bathers.

MEDITATION AND HEALING

Good garden design will ensure that there are places within your garden to sit and rest and which combine well with all the other areas for family activities. You may, however, wish to turn a specific area of your garden into a private sanctuary: a place in which to enjoy fragrance and soothing sounds, to refresh the senses with perhaps a meditation area in which you can recharge your batteries.

The natural world has long been a source of healing. Herbs have been used for centuries for their medicinal powers, and access to a garden is known to aid the recovery of hospital patients, and certainly to help them feel better. So creating a sanctuary in the corner of the garden will help you to clear your mind and relax.

It is possible to design a part of your garden that benefits all five of the human senses. Visual elements are obviously important and should be strong and simple but you can also plan to include soothing sounds and fragrant plants, as well as interesting textures which feel good to the touch and, perhaps, some edible plants.

RIGHT: In the style of a Japanese tea house, this simple, stark pavilion provides a quiet place for contemplation away from the stressful outside world. This type of building was often sited in a quiet place in the garden especially designed for meditation and approached by meandering paths full of mystery and surprise.

ABOVE: The sleek architectural lines of the house are reflected in the deck-level swimming pool and associate well with the uncluttered expanse of the stone terrace. This is all viewed from the swimming pool pavilion at some distance from the house, where low tables and chairs are grouped to form a quiet area for relaxation.

GARDENS FOR THE SENSES

Great pleasure can be derived from looking at something which is pleasing to the eye, so ensure that your area for relaxation has both good internal and external views. Position seats to take in the view of distant hills or a bubbling fountain. Try to cut out eyesores like next door's shed or your washing line and compost bin. And plan the route to your relaxation area especially carefully so that there is a real sense of peace when you arrive and you literally feel your shoulders drop and cares fall away.

Plants must obviously be chosen for their compatibility with the soil and aspect but the colour scheme is also important, as it will determine the atmosphere of the place. A garden full of multicoloured bedding plants, like some municipal parks, will look extremely busy and will feel unrestful.

Strong colours like reds, hot pinks and oranges are colours for warm places, working well in bright sunlight close to a patio, but they may prove too stimulating for true relaxation. Cool, green foliage, however, is exceptionally relaxing and unlike the influence of ephemeral flower colour the calm atmosphere of green plants will last far longer – possibly all year. White flowers combine well with green foliage, and will work towards creating a soothing and refreshing atmosphere, as will the hazy shades of blue and purple.

As with colours, scented plants are a wonderful aid to relaxation as long as there are not too many mixed scents to overpower you. Your selection of plants can be planned carefully to provide scent at different times of the day and year; chimonanthus and some viburnums produce scented winter

flowers while many white-flowered plants, in particular the tobacco plant (*Nicotiana*), have a strong night time scent. A scented arbour can be achieved using climbing roses and honeysuckle, while the structure of your private garden may be made from sweet smelling viburnum, osmanthus and philadelphus. Choisya, cistus and lilac all have fragrant foliage, and can be enjoyed as you sit back with your eyes shut to relax.

It is rarely possible to completely shut out the noise of children, traffic and lawn-mowers. Relaxing music could always be played through a portable stereo or other more soothing sounds could be introduced to take the edge off the more unwelcome noise. Wind blowing gently through birch trees, rustling grasses or bamboo can be soothing as can the gentle tinkling of wind chimes (although these need to be chosen carefully for the right effect). Gentle water features are also well known for their therapeutic effects, although not all are suitable. A crashing waterfall will be too dominant, and the constant tapping of bamboo against stone in a 'Sozu', or Japanese water tipper, can prove excessively irritating. The sound of bees and bird life can be a real pleasure and sensitive planting will attract them into the garden. Buddleia, caryopteris, cornus and lavender are favourites with bees, while shrubs like cotoneaster and elaeagnus will attract birds. A rowan tree could also be planted to entice them in, or you could help your children to make a bird table or nesting box. Birds will also be attracted by shallow splash pools and simple stone bird baths.

In poor light conditions it can be useful and reassuring to walk on textured paving. At other times it can simply be pleasant to walk barefoot on warm bricks and then in cool lush grass or crunchy autumn leaves. Plants pleasing to touch like the crinkle-leafed hornbeam or maybe *Prunus serrula* with its smooth polished bark or the soft woolly-leafed lamb's tongue (*Stachys byzantina*) will add a sensuous dimension to the space. In a cool and shaded garden a variety of mosses will form soft velvety pincushions which are wonderful to touch. Alternatively, the shiny, tight-leafed domes of *Hebe albicans* and box can be used to contrast with softer textures such as a lavender hedge. The tactile characteristics of all these plants bring us closer to the natural world and give us a greater sense of calm.

Most edible plants will be found in the vegetable garden – a place of work, not relaxation. Picking a peach from a warm wall can be wonderful but fruits such as this still require spraying, pollinating and a degree of skill in pruning. Something easier could be tried in the relaxation garden, though, such as thornless loganberries or blackberries, that will scramble over old buildings to produce fruit with a superb taste. You and your children can then experience, once more, the pleasure of picking blackberries from the hedges in late summer. For pure pleasure, what better way to relax than to lie in the cool grass eating alpine strawberries picked in the cool shade of your secluded garden?

HERB GARDENS

If your relaxation garden is in a warm and sheltered position then this is the ideal location for a herb garden. An enclosure of walls or hedges will help to contain the fragrance while the warmth built up within the walls and paving will emanate outwards and benefit the plants. Low box or cotton lavender hedges will keep unruly herbs tidy and provide some structure to the space. This traditional use of low hedges has been used for centuries in herb gardens but you do not necessarily have to stick to the traditional symmetrical style. Asymmetric designs work extremely well with contemporary buildings.

Herb gardens are best positioned close to the house for convenience and a simple fountain providing cool water is a useful addition in a warm, sunny spot. Many herbs are low growing and will not tolerate a heavy soil so it is often best to plant in raised beds; in this way you can fill the beds with well-drained soil and enjoy the fragrance of the plants at close quarters. You could even build in seating possibly planting chamomile to form a soft 'cushion'.

BELOW: Hazy blues and cool greens are always soothing to the eye; here, clipped box, the wispy flowers of catmint, ferns and pink salvias come together in a restful combination of colour and texture.

OPPOSITE: The sight and sound of birds in the garden can be a real pleasure and planting berrying shrubs and trees will help to encourage them. They will also be attracted by a splash pool or simple bird bath.

FAR RIGHT: One of the most soothing sounds which can be introduced into a garden is the hum of bees on a summer's day. Planting buddleia, caryopteris, lavender and salvias will attract bees into the garden.

Alternative uses for herbs

Thyme, oregano and chamomile can all be planted between paving slabs and will release a wonderful fragrance when walked on.

*

Many herbs and dried flowers can be used to make fragrant pot pourri decorations. For a herb leaf pot pourri use mint, sage and thyme. The best time to pick the herbs for drying is early in the morning as soon as the dew has evaporated from the leaves.

*

Herbs can also be used for their medicinal properties. Chamomile tea is excellent for soothing headaches and colds, and chamomile can also be added to the bath for a relaxing soak. Similarly, lavender can be added to hot water and inhaled to help clear head colds, while lemon balm also makes a refreshing and soothing tea.

LEFT: Verbascum towers above lower plants in a herb garden full of varied blues, greys and greens. Herb gardens usually do well in sheltered sunny spots and often make ideal small areas in which to relax; they are probably best positioned close to the house for the convenience of picking herbs from the kitchen.

RIGHT: What simple pleasure it is to walk barefoot on warm textured bricks such as these, and there are few who could resist brushing a hand over the soft lavender hedges to either side of the path.

Many herbs have both a culinary and medicinal value. They are cheap to buy, quick growing, fragrant and many, like bay, artemesia and sage, provide all year evergreen structure. Some plants have a wonderful texture while others such as thyme can be planted underfoot to produce a scented walkway. Most herbs flourish in full sun but others such as the aromatic angelica, chervil with its fern-like leaves and the wild garlic will tolerate dappled shade and be best suited to a cool woodland retreat.

FENG SHUI

The ancient Chinese art of Feng shui has been around for thousands of years and forms part of the trinity of luck or Tien Ti Ren. Heaven luck is your destiny, Feng shui is luck brought through harmony with your environment and Human luck is that which you make for yourself as you go through life. By focusing on the invisible ch'i energy

CONTENTS

RIGHT: The soothing sound of the wind blowing gently through light foliage, trees or rustling grasses and bamboo can be really relaxing. Wind chimes, too, can be restful but ensure that you like the tone of the chime and take care with their position in the garden so they do not to become an irritation rather than a pleasure.

BELOW RIGHT: A trimmed grass path meanders through a summer-flowering meadow of colourful corn cockles and poppies, and leads on to the cooler and darker greens in the background of a hidden and secret garden.

around us, the aim of Feng shui is to put us in harmony with our environment, improving well-being and encouraging a relaxed state of mind. Arranging your garden according to the rules of Feng shui could help to improve your relationships, your health and even your wealth.

The study of Feng shui in the environment around your home must start with a thorough assessment of the site. You should be aiming to create as much good energy as possible in your garden while dispelling any bad energy. The invisible energy, ch'i, can be introduced with soft lines to encourage gentle movement, hidden spaces and areas for rest and relaxation. Ideally your house should be well sited, protected by trees but open at the front. A street heading straight towards your house (as at a T-junction) creates a bad source of energy. You can correct this by planting shrubs to soften the view of the road and other hostile objects

like street lamps. In the same way straight paths are to be avoided in favour of meandering walkways. You also need to create a balance in the garden between the passive energy of yin and the active energy of yang. So here you would need to play down the drama of architectural plants with the soft, more rounded form of others in order to create a balanced picture.

If you are interested in Feng shui you will need to study the bagua or Feng shui map. This map is split into compass points with each point representing a part of your life such as family, education and wealth. Each point is also associated with a colour and a particular element like wood, metal or fire. And it will also have certain garden features or styles linked to that position as well. So, for example, in the south-east corner of your garden associated with the element wood and the colour blue you could construct a wooden compost bin and plant

RIGHT: There is great beauty in the form and line of this Japanese garden; there are no strong colours to offend the eye nor strong movement to cause unrest. The angle of the stone trim is softened by the round form of the clipped box domes while underfoot the cool, green moss forms the perfect carpet.

OPPOSITE: The gardens of the Zen Buddhists were built as symbolic landscapes in order to create an atmosphere of contemplation. Large rocks represent mountains while raked stones portray flowing rivers. It is a style which has been brought through the centuries and today may be incorporated in a corner of a garden simply as a place for calm.

to, we would all then, naturally, be better placed to deal with the rest of our hectic family and working lives.

ZEN GARDENS

Zen Buddhism was introduced to Japan some 800 years ago and had a huge influence on garden styles that can still be seen and appreciated today. In their search for enlightenment the Zen Buddhist priests created small gardens in which to sit and meditate. These small spaces were built as symbolic landscapes into which small trees and rocks were introduced to enhance the atmosphere of contemplation. The gardens were not big statements but were scaled-down representations of the natural world, using large rocks for mountains and raked stone or sand to show vast flowing rivers.

These gardens had an enormous influence on the Japanese people, who had long been crowded into small coastal regions. The high-density population meant that most people had very little land, so they began to develop the limited space in the economic style of Zen gardens as a place in which to escape from the hustle and bustle of urban life. The ritual of tea drinking was also seen as a break from the stressful world and so tea houses were built, too. These were quiet places for contemplation and were approached by meandering paths, full of mystery and surprise, set out asymmetrically, very much in tune with nature. The scaled-down landscapes meant that these meditation gardens were available to everyone and not just to the wealthy landlords of the time.

The possibility of producing a soothing natural landscape in a very small space has also found great popularity in the modern

some blue flowers in order to foster wealth and prosperity.

In recent years Feng shui has been in vogue for the interior of the home and it has now moved outside into the garden where it all began thousands of years ago. However, beware of the hype that surrounds this 'art form'. To create a balanced garden with movement around the space, quiet corners, with eyesores hidden and boundaries softened, is to produce a harmonious environment in which to relax and be at one with nature. Having such a space to escape

Western world. Gardens in the west are very much for outdoor living with areas for entertaining and play, so it is impractical, even in a small family garden, to have the whole area in the Zen style. This style of garden is best suited to one of those awkward corners or to an area that can be screened and hidden from the rest of the garden. The great thing about creating this type of garden is that everyone can appreciate the calm and beauty of such a place regardless of the philosophy behind it.

It certainly helps to create the right atmosphere if you use plants and materials that are in keeping with the Zen style of gardening. You will find it relaxing to sit and look at the wonderful form of a moss-covered rock and listen to the sound of rustling bamboo. Every element introduced into the garden should be chosen for its ability to help you relax and should stimulate your imagination without any distractions. The space may be hidden by bamboo screens or by planting viburnum, nandina or other evergreen shrubs. Small waterfalls, fountains or even a dry river of stones with simple bridges and stepping-stone paths through moss, ajuga or helxine will all contribute to the Zen feel of the place and your own spiritual refreshment.

Planting for Zen gardens

Suitable trees include the stunning Japanese acers, such as *Acer palmatum*, with their incredible autumn colours. *Cercidiphyllum japonicum* also has wonderful autumn colour although young leaves can be damaged by frost. Birch trees also work well in this style of garden, especially *Betula papyrifera* with its striking peeling white bark.

*

Shrubs and bamboo form the main planting in these small spaces. Arundinaria provides good background planting, with the tall arching stems of *Arundinaria murieilae* giving good screening and great sound effects as the leaves rustle in the breeze. There are also numerous evergreen cotoneasters suitable for background screening including the arching variety *Cotoneaster salicifolius* 'Rothschildianus'. The viburnum family includes evergreens like *Viburnum tinus* for screening and deciduous, fragrant varieties such as *V.* x *juddii* as well as the winter-flowering *V. farreri*. *Enkianthus campanulatus* is another tall, deciduous shrub with cream-coloured, bell-shaped flowers in spring. However, it does require an acid soil. Other acid-soil plants include all the azaleas. They come as tall deciduous varieties or compact evergreens, and all of them provide the wonderful colours of a Japanese woodland garden – as does *Photinia* x *fraseri* 'Red Robin' with its young red leaves that turn a dark glossy green when mature.

DECKCHAIR COVER

Bring new life to your faded deckchair by creating this easy-to-make tie-on cover. Do not remove the existing fabric from the chair, as this is stapled on to the wooden frame and forms a strong seat, and use it as a template for the size of your new cover. The cover is made with a tie at each corner so that it can easily be fixed on to the deckchair and just as easily removed for washing or to turn it over for a different look. The cover can be made with two good sides so that it is reversible, which prevents one side from fading too quickly and gives you an alternative look for your garden furniture. You could, in fact, make several covers and have 'new' furniture throughout the summer.

BELOW: In the midst of far more expensive garden furniture, the classic deckchair stands out as being great value for money in terms of both comfort and style; it stores flat and can be carried out easily into the garden.

OPPOSITE: This simple-to-make tie-on cover, which can be removed easily for washing, will give your old deckchair a new lease of life.

MATERIALS
* Piece of fabric the same size as the existing deckchair cover plus seam allowance
* Second piece of fabric as above plus sufficient to make up four ties as described opposite
* Thread

TOOLS
* Sewing machine
* Tape measure
* Pins
* Scissors
* Needle
* Iron

1 Choose two complementary pieces of cotton fabric of equal weight and cut out a piece from each to the same size as the existing deckchair seat, allowing for seams of about 2.5cm (1in) all round the edges.

2 From the remaining fabric, cut out four rectangles each measuring 54cm x 9cm (21½in x 3½in). With the right sides together fold each one in half lengthways, pin and sew, with a seam allowance all round of 2.5cm (1in), to make four ties. Leave a gap so that the ties can be turned the right way out, and after trimming back the seam allowance do just that. Slip stitch the remaining opening and press with an iron on the right side.

3 Pin the ties, folded in half, to the right side of one of your pieces of fabric. Place the right side of other fabric on top and sew the seams, catching the ties and leaving a side opening to turn through.

4 Slip stitch the opening, press and tie the cover on to the deckchair over the existing seat. Your new cover can be removed for washing and ironing and you can ring the changes by using the other side. Before use and after washing, the new cover could be sprayed with a waterproofing, stain-resisting product to help prolong its use and keep it looking crisp.

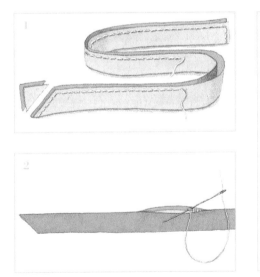

WALL-MOUNTED FOUNTAIN

This is one of the simplest water features to install in your garden and yet it can be extremely effective. The lion's head mask is just one of many fountain heads available from a wide variety, including a spouting lizard which looks particularly good when set among exotic foliage. A free-standing garden wall or an outhouse wall makes the ideal support for this feature, as the water pipe can pass up the back of the wall without any problem. This is obviously not so easy if the fountain is to be fixed to the house wall or to a wall adjacent to your neighbour's garden. In either of these cases it may be easier to run the pipework up the face of the wall and mask it with planting. Some fountain masks and reservoir bowls are available as a self-contained unit and can simply be fixed to the face of any wall, as there is no separate connecting pipe to be fitted. The tank that holds the water and houses the pump may be set in the ground or, as in this example, it is a stone trough that actually sits on the ground. In both cases, pebbles are held over the water by a metal grid that hides the pump and makes this a safe feature, as there is no open surface of water. Choose the pump for the feature according to the supplier's recommendation. Most pumps for this type of fountain will need only a low-voltage power supply and should therefore be connected through a transformer to the mains. Large pumps and other electrical fittings in the garden which are powered by mains electricity will always need a circuit breaker fitted; if you are in any doubt about electrical installation, seek the help of a qualified electrician.

MATERIALS

* Old stone trough
* 8 bricks
* Lion's head mask
* 4 rustproof screws and wall plugs or 1 coach screw
* Length of flexible pipe
* Wire mesh to support pebbles
* One bag of beach pebbles
* Low-voltage submersible pump
* Additional electrical cable (if necessary)
* Waterproof junction box (if necessary)
* Transformer

TOOLS

* Spade
* Power drill and masonry bits
* Spirit level
* Wire strippers
* Screwdriver
* Pencil

1 Set the stone trough level against the front of the wall and mark two holes on the wall for the inlet and outlet pipes. The inlet hole will be found by holding the lion's mask in the correct position and marking the point in the wall where the pipe will come into the back of the mask. The outlet hole will be directly below this and just above the rim of the stone trough. Put bricks into the trough as shown which will later support the grid.

2 After drilling through the wall, push a length of flexible pipe through the outlet hole, extending it up the back of the wall and then through the inlet hole. Fix the mask itself either by a screw in each corner or by hanging it on a strong coach screw fixed to the wall.

3 Place the submersible pump in position and connect the outlet pipe. Run the cable over the

rear edge of the trough and then fit the grid, which may have to be cut to size. Then support the grid on bricks to hold it above the pump, but it should be about 5cm (2in) down from the top of the trough to support the pebbles.

4 Either take the cable through a hole drilled in the house wall, or if the water feature is at some distance from the house then connect the cable in a waterproof junction box to an additional length of cable. This cable must either be heavy-duty armoured cable or it must be run through a conduit back to the house. Connect the cable through a transformer to the mains supply. Fill the stone trough with water and switch on the pump to test it. You can adjust the flow of the water by turning a small tap on the top of the pump. When you are satisfied that the flow is correct, switch off the pump and cover the grid with pebbles. You may need to run the pump again and make a final adjustment to the position of the pebbles to ensure that the water does not splash over the sides of the trough and empty the system.

OPPOSITE: When choosing a water feature for a young family garden, safety must be the first priority. Water bubbling up through pebbles or splashing down into a hidden reservoir are both safe and effective features.

ABOVE: The spouting mask is one of the simplest ways in which to introduce moving water into a garden. This particular example requires no excavation for a reservoir and so simplifies the task still further.

ARBOUR

An arbour is a shaded retreat, possibly with a built-in bench, where you can sit and relax while enjoying views out over the garden. Constructions such as these are often situated to form a strong focal point, leading out to your secret garden retreat where fragrant climbing roses, honeysuckle or jasmine may be planted to grow over the arbour to enhance the relaxed atmosphere. This arbour or niche is based on a seventeenth-century design and may be used either as an open canopy or enclosed by planting such as clipped hornbeam. The curved elements would need to be prepared by a joinery workshop and then assembled with the straight timbers in your garden. Good quality, pressure-treated softwood would be fine for this construction, with an application of decorative woodstain to complete the job. The arbour could be positioned over a small paved seating area and set among a background of shrubs.

This arbour based on a seventeenth-century design, nestles under a canopy of overhanging branches to create a small, shaded retreat. The pale blue woodstain tones well with the surrounding foliage while the ball finial is a stylish addition which completes the structure.

MATERIALS

* Timber (pressure-treated softwood:
  18 quadrants 70cm x 7.5cm x 5cm
  (28in x 3in x 2in)
  9 straight pieces 105cm x 7.5cm x
  5cm (42in x 3in x2in)
* Trellis 19.2m (63ft) standard
  roof tilers' lath
* 4 pointed timber stakes 60cm x
  10cm x 10cm (24in x 4in x 4in)
* Nails and screws, rustproof:
  20 wood screws 10cm (4in) long
  70 wood screws 5cm (2in) long
  80 round-headed wire nails 5cm
  (2in) long
* 1 litre waterproof PVA wood glue
* 2.5 litres decorative wood stain

TOOLS

* Hand saw
* Electric drill with
  screwdriver and drill bits
* Claw hammer
* Chisels
* Workbench
* Adjustable angle
  marker and square
* Spirit level
* Crowbar
* Sledge hammer
* Paint brushes

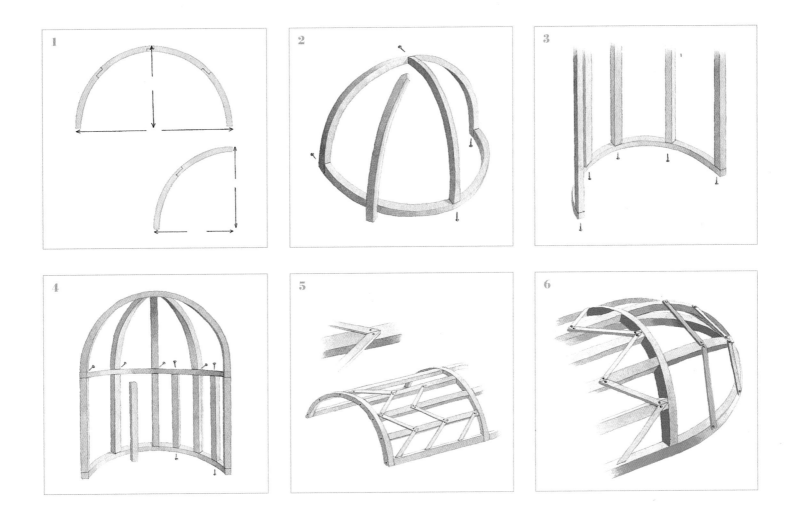

1 There are three semicircles of wood used in the construction of this arbour together with three quadrants, all of which can be prepared beforehand in a joinery workshop. The half lap joints can either be cut for you by the same workshop or you can attempt to do this yourself – it is quite simple. Each half lap joint should then be assembled using two 5cm (2in) wood screws and some wood glue.

2 Construct the top semi-dome structure by screwing two of the semicircles together at right angles using 10cm (4in) wood screws and wood glue. Fit the central quadrant using the same method, followed by the two other quadrants which must be given angled cuts so that they fit neatly at the top.

3 Screw the five main upright timbers, which are 105cm (42in) long into position from underneath the base semicircle using 10cm (4in) wood screws and wood glue.

4 Position the semi-dome on to the uprights and screw it down with five 10cm (4in) wood screws, diagonally through the base of the semi-dome into the upright timbers. Then screw the intermediate posts into position, from above and below, between each of the main upright timbers.

5 In order to fix the trellis laths, you will need to lay the arbour down on its front. To fit the lower section trellis, first nail and glue a piece of lath 105cm (42in) long to the inside edge of the two front posts. Then construct the diagonal pattern trelliswork by cutting sections of lath to the required length and nailing them on to the back of the posts.

6 Cut two horizontal rows of trellis laths to the required length and nail them on to the back of the semi-dome. Finish the whole construction by applying one or two coats of decorative wood stain. Finally, secure the arbour into position by driving wooden stakes down into the ground behind the structure and screwing through the stakes into the base ring.

the cookes, **relaxed living**

Eleven years ago Michael and Cathy Cooke moved into Hawthorne Stud in Central Mangrove on the New South Wales central coast. They had been searching for a property near to Sydney and their workplaces which would also give them room for their horses. Hawthorne Stud was ideal, although it took imagination to see its potential through the uncleared scrub that greeted them.

There are five acres of land at Hawthorne Stud, three for the horses and two for the garden, lying at the top of a ridge overlooking the blue mountains to the south west. The summers here are hot and dry and the winters are short and mild, so the garden plays a vital role for the family all throughout the year.

The Cookes inherited little or no garden to speak of but instead a desolate area of land which was littered with old earth-moving machinery and broken concrete. Even weeds could barely get a hold in the deep sandy soil, which supported only a few scraggly fruit trees and the native gum trees that still stand throughout the plot, giving strength and maturity to the garden.

ABOVE: Lighting is used to extend the hours of entertaining and add a magical ingredient to this garden.

OPPOSITE: One of Michael's and Nathan's favourite places is the jetty down by the lake; the hammock is great for snoozing in on hot days.

BELOW: An open gate entices you to explore this lush part of the garden.

ABOVE: The Cooke's spacious garden allows a mixture of styles to be introduced which work well together, from ornamental grasses to clipped hedges and topiary through to native planting and the paddock beyond.

Michael's initial layout for the garden was influenced by the early part of his career as a nurseryman, with collections of rare plants being grown as a source of material for his nursery business. As his interest and business in garden design grew, so the garden developed a stronger layout and changed from a nursery stock ground to a family garden in which to relax, play and entertain friends. As the garden and plants have matured, with help from daily barrowloads of stable manure, the space has also changed from just a hot and windy site to an area of different microclimates. Areas within the garden have become well sheltered from the drying winds and some are really quite shaded and moist, allowing a vast range of different plants to flourish.

The garden is a wonderful outdoor room made up of many different areas: a driveway lined with autumn-berrying shrubs, split-level lawns with thick shrub planting and a recently built stone terrace for entertaining, with pergolas and an open fireplace. Michael's favourite area lies to the front of the house and comprises a variety of ornamental grasses whose colours and appearance change constantly with the seasons. There is a very pretty orchard with fruit trees and rose bushes where the occasional chicken can be seen running around. There is also a 30m (100ft) lake fed by winter rain which is home to ducks and grebes and all kinds of other water birds and frogs. The banks down to the water are carpeted in rough grass while at one end of the lake is a covered jetty where Michael and his five-year-old son, Nathan, can be found snoozing in the hammock on hot days, if not swimming in the lake.

Another favourite spot is the balcony where Michael and Cathy entertain their friends under the shade of a eucalyptus tree. It is a perfect vantage point from which to view the garden and oversee Nathan and his young friends playing in the treehouse, on the trampoline and on the swings and slides. It is very much a family garden, in which to play games, pick fresh fruit and have picnics on the

These ornamental grasses, which change colour with the seasons, are growing at the front of the house and form Michael's favourite area within the garden.

Dense tree and shrub planting forms a backdrop to a more open area with strong accent plants and contrasting soft clipped domes.

The stone hearth at the front of the open fireplace makes an ideal seat where Michael and his son can sit and read.

jetty. When Nathan is home from school he is free to run round the whole garden with the dogs or shower under the sprinklers. Only the gate down to the lake is kept locked while he is so young.

Michael spends most of his spare time in the garden or with the horses, which Cathy trains for the show ring. Both of them are keen riders. Cathy also likes decorating and so the interior of the house, which was completely rebuilt, changes as often as finances allow.

Michael and Cathy spent a long time searching for the perfect old place to move into before they found Hawthorne Stud. When they first moved in, the property was not conducive to relaxed living, and it has taken years of hard work to establish the garden that they wanted. It is Nathan who has made them relax in the environment they have created. Initially, Michael planted rare plants and was forever changing things around and now, with Nathan flying around the garden, that cannot be done and they naturally spend more time with him and less time rearranging plants.

Ground rules

* *A garden put to good use is more important than how it looks.*

* *Take time to observe and enjoy the fine details and subtleties within a garden.*

* *Work with the microclimates in your garden.*

* *Create interest through diversity of plant material.*

* *A spacious garden allows for a variety of complementary styles to be introduced.*

* *Plant for seasonal interest so that a garden will follow its natural cycle.*

The jetty by the lake is a great place for observing the vast array of wildlife and, of course, for enjoying the hammock.

The treehouse is just one of the many places where Nathan and his young friends can play in the garden at Hawthorne Stud.

While Nathan continues to charge around exploring, the Cookes have learnt to spend more time relaxing in the garden they have created.

the cummings, **relaxed village life**

The small village of Penallt sits on a ridge between the Usk and Wye valleys, near the Welsh border town of Monmouth. It is an area of wonderful natural habitats with an abundance of wildlife, but close enough to good motorway links to provide access to work. It is the location of the home of Cheryl Cummings, a successful garden designer, and her husband David, which is the epitome of relaxed living – mown paths wander through wild flower meadows next to flowing curved lawns, and a swing hangs idly under a large sycamore tree. The house, which is light and spacious, sits to the east of a low hill where it bathes in glorious morning light; that same hill does hide the last of the setting sun but also provides protection by sheltering the garden from the strong westerly winds. The house has been softened with shrubs and climbers while the whole garden, with its meadow and secluded sitting areas, has developed a very special atmosphere of freedom.

ABOVE: Flowing lawns and mown paths through wild flower meadows have helped to give this garden a free and relaxed atmosphere.

LEFT AND BELOW LEFT: The garden had not been cultivated for 12 years when the Cummings moved here, which fortunately meant that this wonderful flowering meadow had remained undisturbed.

OPPOSITE: Some of the lower rocks which were installed to retain an existing steep bank make an ideal seat where Cheryl can relax surrounded by the soft alchemilla, verbena and towering foxgloves.

When David and Cheryl moved here seven years ago, they took on a garden which had not been touched by their predecessors for twelve years! This was probably a blessing as the wild meadow in the front garden was undisturbed, and Cheryl had a blank canvas to develop her own design for the garden. The garden was designed to accommodate a laid-back attitude to its ongoing maintenance.

Cheryl is, according to David, obsessed with gardens. Her own garden, though, is a place for relaxation and she will often unwind by sitting at the water's edge listening to the birds. David, on the other hand, is a company director, not a gardener. He reads the paper in the garden for relaxation, while his active gardening stretches only to picking nasturtium leaves for Iggy, the pet iguana. Their two teenage children also enjoy the garden. Their son, John, entertains his friends there, while Rhiannon, their daughter, can be seen, on occasion, fishing in the pond or watching birds.

When the Cummings first moved in they found some problems: the house had been cut into the hillside, leaving a steep grass bank which was impossible to maintain while the heavy, compacted clay over underlying rock caused frequent flooding, including of the garage. The rocks that were used to retain the steep bank and the pond were all introduced out of necessity but have now become strong focal points. A random paved terrace was constructed overlooking a dry stream of pebbles leading to the pond and rock bank. The pebbles help to keep the soil warm, allowing plants such as grasses, alliums and *Verbena bonariensis* to flourish.

Much of the initial planting was introduced to provide structure, to screen the road and to create hidden depths in the narrower parts of the garden. Cheryl has experimented with different planting, fine-tuning the scheme to see what combinations work well, which has also been useful research for her work.

A secret garden accessible only by a gateway provides the perfect relaxing retreat from the hustle and bustle of everyday life.

Pebbles lead from the lawn through yellow-flowering alchemilla, which has been allowed to spread and soften the stones surrounding the circular pool.

Cheryl designed the garden to be used by everyone in the family, and certainly over the years the children have enjoyed playing in the front meadow, riding bicycles around the trees and building dens in the thick shrub planting. The garden has been used for barbecue parties and family meals on the terrace, but, above all the garden is a place for relaxation in which to stroll and enjoy the quiet, peaceful atmosphere.

Cheryl's philosophy has always been to go with nature, not to fight it nor to be obsessive about removing weeds, in fact she takes comfort in the knowledge that if ever stung by a nettle there will always be a dockleaf close by. David and Cheryl now spend as much spare time as possible relaxing in the garden, as children's parties have given way to quiet drinks for two. In Cheryl's words, a bottle of chilled wine on a summer's evening, watching the house martins flying high in the sky, just cannot be beaten.

Ground rules

* *Work with nature, do not fight it.*

* *Enjoy the natural habit of plants – do not stake, tie or prune them into submission.*

* *Plan for wildlife as birds will bring life, colour and interest to the dullest of days.*

* *Choose the hard construction materials carefully to suit the site so that your garden blends comfortably with the surrounding landscape.*

The tall grass, *Stipa gigantea*, fennel and buddleia frame the random stone terrace and bench which has been positioned to catch the sun.

A boulder once used by the Cummings' son John for an art project has now become a focal point among dense planting.

entertaining

ENTERTAINING

The great outdoors can provide the perfect setting

ABOVE: Coastal gardens are often wonderful settings for entertaining with panoramic views and invigorating sea air. Here the dining area is sited in the lower, more sheltered position where the parasol offers shade over the table, while the toughened glass panels provide shelter from sea breezes and allow uninterrupted views to the horizon.

The patio has become the most social area in our gardens today – an outdoor extension of living rooms where you can gather together friends for a lunchtime barbecue, entertain guests at an evening dinner party or host an impromptu drinks party. Patios and raised terraces can now be easily constructed from a vast array of materials, including natural stone, pre-cast concrete slabs and timber decking, making it easier than ever to select a style that complements not only your house and garden but also your lifestyle.

for a great time for everyone whatever their age.

Patios are usually set close to the house for convenience but they can be sited further away to catch the sun or enjoy a view, remaining connected to the house by a hard paved pathway or a timber boardwalk. A roof terrace enjoying stunning bird's-eye views can be used in the same way, making a spectacular place for entertaining.

All of these areas will need a degree of shelter from the elements. Low shrub planting around patios will give protection against chill breezes while permeable barriers like slatted timber are a good choice of screening for roof gardens. Parasols and awnings offer welcome shade and a timber pergola with twining vines gives a wonderful dappled effect. A solid roof over the veranda will protect your dinner guests from a summer shower while its open sides will allow you to enjoy the experience of outdoor eating.

Lawns are often the largest outdoor area for entertaining, providing a soft, safe surface for children's parties or large-scale weddings and anniversaries. Lawns are also great for picnics – the simple pleasure of sitting down to eat in the shade of a spreading tree is hard to beat. As with picnics, barbecues are one of the easiest outdoor parties to organise.

Furniture should be chosen with looks, durability and comfort in mind. Some furniture may be permanent and a feature in its own right while other pieces may be portable for ease of movement around the garden and for easy storage when not in use.

The conservatory is the link between indoors and outdoors, where materials such as bricks, tiles and flagstones can extend from the house out on to the patio. Plants also form a visual link with those in the garden, and the warm conditions of a conservatory will enable you to grow certain varieties that are simply too tender to be grown outside. Lighting in the garden allows you to extend your entertaining beyond the hours of daylight and subtle, low-level lights will guide your party guests around the garden while candles on the table will create that special, intimate atmosphere.

Creating the right environment for entertaining requires good design, while the organisation of the entertainment itself – the picnics, barbecues and other parties – relies on sensitive planning. If you get this right then you will be able to entertain easily and really enjoy outdoor living.

PATIOS AND TERRACES

ABOVE: Patios are often sited close to the house so that indoor living rooms can flow straight into the outdoor living area. Peering out into the bright sunlight, the two little dogs in this garden look out from the cool darkness of the house to the warm shingle patio decorated with pots of brightly coloured flowers.

OPPOSITE: A circular stone table with simple chairs under the dappled shade of a tree forms an imaginative patio area with a good view back to the house. The random stones set into the grass provide a firm, dry surface but with a soft outline which blends more easily into the surrounding garden.

If the kitchen has become the focus of family life inside the home then the patio has become the centre for outdoor living. The terms patio and terrace have now become synonymous although technically a terrace is a level sitting area that is raised above the surrounding landscape. A paved area such as this, supported by retaining walls or planted banks with steps sweeping down to a lawn at a lower level, can be most effective. The word patio, on the other hand, originated in Spain and was used to describe an open, tiled inner courtyard. It has since come to mean any paved area in a garden used for entertaining.

A patio tends, on the whole, to lead out from the house so that indoor living areas join straight on to the outdoor living area, with the added convenience of proximity to the kitchen for the preparation and serving of food. Patios adjacent to the house also prevent mud from being trampled indoors and they provide a firm, level surface for tables and chairs.

Housing developers will usually build a patio at the back of the house even if this is a cold and shaded position. With a little imagination a much more useful area can be built further away in a sunny spot, linked to the house by a paved pathway. Even if you already have a large, paved area constructed you can make it more interesting by dividing it up into intimate enclosed spaces for outdoor meals at different times

of the day. A small breakfast patio surrounded by planting may lead out on to a larger paved area for family meals and dinner parties, which is linked to a secluded space to catch the evening sun for a quiet supper. In your garden you could plan in a series of linked paved areas away from the house to enjoy sunshine at different times of the day. The position of the main terrace for dinner parties is less dependent on the movement of the sun as its greatest use will be for dining in the evening.

Front and side gardens are often overlooked as entertaining areas and certainly if you live next to a busy street they are impractical. However, if you are lucky enough to live in a secluded setting with the best aspect to the front of the house then you may consider making your prime entertaining area here. Suitable shrub planting can always conceal the path to the front door and cars parked on the driveway.

PLANNING

Patios and terraces need to be planned carefully. They should be in proportion with the house and the garden and you need to ensure that they allow sufficient room for your family and guests to move around in comfort. If you like entertaining or have a large family, be generous with the amount of space you plan for your tables and chairs, making sure that there is sufficient room for chairs to be pulled out without falling into

surrounding plants. If you are a couple who have small parties then close the space down and make a more intimate setting, as a small table set in a sea of paving can feel uncomfortable and will look ridiculous. Use the space well, making sure that all areas are accessible and that there are no dead corners that cannot be used.

Good, broad openings from the house on to the patio are essential so that your guests do not have to fight their way through leaves, branches and plants to reach the dinner table. Low perimeter walls around the patio are unnecessary and take up a lot of space as they are invariably double thickness, containing a narrow planter. Such walls are reminiscent of the parapets and balustrading around the raised terraces of grand gardens where their aim was to protect guests from falling over the edge. In this context they make sense, but in smaller gardens a low free-standing wall bordering a patio is simply a nuisance, doing nothing to soften the patio edge and succeeding only in cutting off the rest of the garden from it. It is far better to include some low, softening planting at each side, to create a smooth, broad and uninterrupted link from the patio to the lawn.

Even on a raised terrace, unless it is very high or very grand, there is not always the need for balustrading or perimeter walls; low planting will keep you away from the edge and provide a far softer link with the rest of the garden. However, where the ground around the patio slopes upwards you

may need a surrounding low wall, although this is really a retaining wall. This type of wall is far more useful as it provides built-in seating backed and protected by layers of terraced planting. Sitting in areas that are partly enclosed by planting, whether on terraces or at ground level, always feels more comfortable than being isolated in a barren paved area. You can also add atmosphere to eating areas by surrounding them with fragrant Mediterranean plants like cistus, lavender, salvias and rosemary, all of which help to set the scene for successful and enjoyable entertaining.

PRACTICALITIES

A successful paved area relies on a sound base of slabs laid on a bed of mortar (sand and cement) over a sub-base of compacted hardcore. Build a patio that will last for years and do not be tempted to cut corners and cost by laying slabs on sand over compacted earth, as you will only end up with an uneven and dangerous surface.

OPPOSITE: Sufficient room to sit comfortably at the table while still permitting uninterrupted movement through the space is needed on a patio. Here an intimate area has been created for a table and two chairs with ample room to pass by on the deck and out under the pergola.

ABOVE: Access from the patio to the lawn is at either side of an area of low planting, which gives a sense of enclosure but still allows uninterrupted views of the garden.

If you have any doubts about your building abilities then you should employ a reputable landscape contractor to deal with the construction.

Aim for the finished level of your paving to be 15cm (6in or two courses of brickwork) below the damp-proof course (dpc) in your house wall and lay your paving with a slight fall across the patio to take surface water away from the house into surrounding beds. New houses always seem to have drain covers set in the most prominent position, but you can get around this problem by setting slabs into special recessed covers or by planting ground cover shrubs close by which will, in time, spread over and mask the drain cover. Never use containers to try to hide the drain cover as that will only serve to draw attention to it.

Paved areas need to be kept simple, avoiding too many fussy patterns which can be hard to get right without it all looking too contrived. To keep the cutting of slabs to a minimum, consider leaving the edge of the patio as a staggered line to be softened by shrubs rather than laboriously trying to cut a curved edge. Small-unit paving like bricks or setts can be used to fill in the staggered end of a paved patio if a curved line is desired.

Crisp, geometric patterns work well with contemporary designs but they create a fairly static picture, whereas staggering the slabs will create a greater sense of movement. Paving stones laid in a completely random pattern produce the most satisfactory results when laying natural and imitation natural stone slabs. With this type of paving the occasional small slab or mortar joint is left out and low creeping herbs like thyme – which can withstand being trodden

LEFT: This rugged terrace exudes great strength in design and construction and makes the perfect outdoor room. The wide area of warm-coloured, natural stone allows plenty of room for entertaining and if there is a large party then extra seats can be brought in to add to the stone bench by the fireplace and the two wooden chairs. The pillars and beams with canvas drapes, here to provide shelter from the hot Australian sun, create a comfortable feeling of enclosure. In such a setting, Mediterranean shrubs like cistus and lavender would work well, together with herbs such as rosemary and oregano.

97

LEFT: This small, enclosed patio or garden room makes an intimate setting for eating outdoors, at the same time enjoying the open air and yet remaining sheltered, too. The supporting posts for the enclosure, which are connected by diamond trellis with climbing plants, also serve to frame the views out into the garden. The low parapet wall between two of the posts makes a perfect ledge for pot plants and doubles up as an occasional seat.

RIGHT: This large and sunny terrace illustrates clearly the importance of adequate space around a table, allowing chairs to be pulled back easily and guests to sit in comfort. The terrace also has uninterrupted access on to the lawn and clear views of the surrounding landscape.

on – can be planted in the gaps for their fragrance. Planting is essential to soften and break up the harsh lines of paving, especially against the house wall. New patios always finish flush against the back of the wall of the house, when really a planting pocket about 60cm (2ft) wide would be preferable. This allows you to plant shrubs and climbers to form a soft break between the hard horizontal and vertical surfaces.

STYLE AND MATERIALS

The materials that you choose for your patio and terrace need to be in keeping with the style of your garden and house. Natural stone paving or good imitation pre-cast concrete form ideal surfaces with the addition of brick trim or insets to link up with the house walls. Textured paving provides an excellent flat, non-slip surface that is especially useful around water and if you have young children. Some riven paving is just too uneven and may cause garden furniture to wobble and youngsters to trip, so choose carefully. Small paving units like bricks will look wonderful when laid in a courtyard garden but over a large patio the overall picture may be too fussy.

Natural stone flags are usually best if bought new; reclaimed paving is available but its quality is often questionable. If it has been lifted from the floors of disused factories its surface may well have been spoilt by tar and oil stains, which will seep out in hot weather. These paving stones can also be incredibly thick, making them difficult to lay, whereas you will be able to specify an even thickness for new paving.

Concrete slabs that look like brick paving are not to be recommended and neither are slabs in gaudy colours; muted natural stone colours will usually work best in a garden. Other disasters to be avoided include printed concrete. This is a smooth, coloured concrete with patterns of paving slabs imprinted on its surface. The overall appearance is shiny and artificial and very often the method of construction is unreliable. Admittedly, it is mainly used for driveways but it has also been used for patios. Another driveway material that is often wrongly used for patios is concrete block paving, usually laid to a herringbone pattern. This material really is better suited to supermarket car parks and garage forecourts than to elegant terraces for dinner parties. For flowing curved areas concrete can be laid with a brushed aggregate finish. After laying the concrete, it should be allowed to set almost hard before brushing and watering the surface to leave a stony, textured finish. It really is quite a skilled job to get the timing and technique right and is something that is best left to professionals. When done well the overall appearance can be effective and, of course, the textured surface is ideal next to a pool. The finish can be just a bit too rough for a patio and it is probably best suited to utility as opposed to entertaining areas.

A more up-to-date solution is resin-bonded aggregate which produces an altogether finer, textured surface and a very smart, crisp appearance. It is a mix of fine aggregates and resin, which is laid to form a hard surface with an even better texture for grip. It looks best if laid between a pattern of brick bands and is again a technique best left to a good contractor.

Natural stone setts in granite or sandstone are wonderful for paving small patios or to lay as a pattern or edging detail within larger areas of natural stone paving. Both materials will give a slightly uneven surface and so are not best suited to large dining tables, but they do work well on a small, secluded breakfast terrace. There are also some very good pre-cast concrete setts on the market; these are not only cheaper but also have a more even surface.

Terracotta tiles form a beautiful, warm paved surface, but unless you live in a Mediterranean climate they are probably best used in the conservatory or kitchen where they are safe from damaging frosts. However, some brilliant imitation terracotta tiles in pre-cast concrete are now available

RIGHT: Random-sized flagstones with grass joints look just right in this very simple patio which blends perfectly with its surroundings. Grass can be very effective when allowed to grow in the paving joints as it can be mown straight over and links well with adjacent lawn areas. Low creeping herbs also work well in sunny positions, releasing their fragrance when trodden on.

OPPOSITE BELOW: Patios look particularly good when enclosed by planting and set at some distance from the house. The terrace in this woodland clearing has been laid in bricks, which are an extremely useful paving material as their small unit size allows them to be laid to curves and to soft outlines. Bricks are also warm underfoot and often have a rough texture to give extra grip, which is especially important when laid close to water or in semi-shade.

and you will find it hard to tell them from the genuine article. These tiles can be used to extend visually the flooring in your kitchen or dining room out into the garden, thus providing an excellent link between indoor and outdoor living.

Decking is certainly the surface of the moment in the United Kingdom, although in California as well as other parts of the world where timber is readily available for construction and the climate is warm, decking has been around for a very long time. Perhaps the climate of Northern

Europe is changing for the better both in terms of the weather and in our attitude to design and outdoor living.

Television programmes and garden shows have had an incredible influence on the public's understanding and acceptance of decking as a suitable material for terraces. Timber is, after all, a softer and warmer material to walk on than concrete paving and looks far more sympathetic in a landscape setting. Like all materials, though, it will only look right and be suitable for certain locations and unfortunately

surface of the deck boards, which helps to give a good grip. Dirt is likely to become trapped in the grooves over time and the deck will need washing out periodically to prevent this. All timber should be cleaned at least once or twice a year with a hose or jetwash. (Whether it is timber or a paved surface that you are washing down, take care with cleaning fluids that may cause damage to surrounding plants.) Bearing safety in mind, especially if you have young children, you may need to consider some sort of balustrading around the deck, particularly if it is sited next to water or raised at some height above ground level. Keep the design of this balustrade as simple as possible as it is there to lean on and to give protection rather than as a focal point.

There is an obvious association between decks and water so they are ideal where entertaining areas link with swimming pools, spas and water features. The deck boards look just right, are warm under bare feet and are also free draining. Where decks extend over planted banks, some of the mature plants can be allowed to grow through openings cut in the surface – an

its success and popularity has inevitably led to its misuse. A plethora of decking companies have appeared over the last few years, many of which do not provide adequate advice to prospective customers.

The main concerns expressed about decking are the likelihood of it becoming dangerous and slippery and the possibility of the timber becoming green with algae in shady conditions. A sunny location is essential and decks under heavy shade are not to be recommended. You can now buy timber with small grooves milled into the

effect that can look stunning, especially when light foliage trees such as silver birch (*Betula pendula*) grow up through the deck to cast their dappled shade over the area. Decks can be constructed for streamlined minimalist gardens or surrounded by silver foliage plants for Mediterranean and sunny Californian gardens; a dense surround of lush-leafed plants can also be introduced for an altogether more tropical atmosphere.

There are various types of timber that you can consider using, with treated soft-wood being the cheapest and one of the easiest to work with. There are so many soft-woods from which to choose but some of them may be full of knots and prone to splinter, so it is well worth looking at samples before making your choice. Hardwoods are at the other end of the scale, often being very expensive, but they will last a long time and do not need treating. One of the best decking timbers around is western red cedar, known just as cedar. This timber has a very tight grain, is not prone to splintering and has an in-built resin which means there is no need for additional preservative. To keep costs down you could consider using cedar for the deck and a cheaper softwood for the hidden construction of supporting posts and beams below. Also, do make sure that the timber originates from managed forests.

In addition to new timber you may find a good source of reclaimed timber, which might be more suitable for a small jetty over a pool in a more relaxed setting. Old railway sleepers have been used for timber surfaces, but I think that their best use is reserved for retaining banks in low-use parts of the garden as they are prone to weeping tar in hot weather.

LEFT: Decking provides a wonderful warm material for this open sunny terrace and pool surround. The clean lines of the deck have been softened by clumps of ornamental grasses, which form a neat band around the entertaining area and a soft edge to the woods in the background. Open expanses of decking in cedar or good quality treated softwood look superb next to water, perhaps with some dappled shade from light foliage trees such as silver birch.

ROOF TERRACES

tions and the danger of outdoor living in such a lofty position. When roof gardens are designed into a new building an allowance can be made to include wide-span structural supports for the terrace and suitable waterproofing for raised beds. What you can do with a terrace on an older building may be more limited or, indeed, an unknown quantity altogether. A structural engineer should always be engaged to advise you on what you can and cannot do, but even they may not commit themselves to suggesting any more than 'minimum additions' unless they can see clearly the hidden roof construction beneath the terrace.

The weight of a roof terrace really is an issue so minimise the problem by choosing lightweight materials and spreading the weight. If the terrace is supported by two load-bearing walls, which extend upwards to form the side walls to your roof terrace, they could be used as supports for decking joists. In this case, the decking actually becomes a suspended floor and takes the weight off the roof itself. The timber theme can be continued with the construction of seats and planting boxes that can be secured to the walls. Containers should be made of lightweight fibreglass, filled with free-draining compost – not heavy soil – and additional fibreglass rocks that look as good as the real thing. Choosing furniture for these lofty sites can often be a problem as gusting winds will tend to blow light-

ABOVE: A wide canvas parasol offers protection over the sitting area in this roof garden, while timber decking has been used successfully to surface the floor. Deck joists which span from one wall to another take the weight off the roof itself and the deck then actually becomes a suspended floor.

Terraces that are set among the roof tops tend to be in the centre of a city where garden space is either limited or belongs to the ground floor apartment. This means that the views enjoyed from the roof terrace are often of spectacular city skylines, making them a very stylish environment for entertaining family and friends.

The pleasures of a roof terrace must be hard earned as gardens that are set at some height above ground level are not without inherent problems – namely exposure to high winds and light levels, weight limita-

LEFT: Roof terraces may
be small but they often
enjoy spectacular views, in
this case the London
skyline. The pleasures of
such a position can be hard
earned though as roof-top
gardens may not be
without inherent problems
including high light
levels, gusting winds and
weight restrictions.
A safety barrier is obviously
essential, too, either
toughened glass or a
slatted screen are
generally the best options.

weight furniture around. Solid teak or cast iron chairs could certainly stay out all year without being moved but may be too heavy for the roof. A solution may be to choose lightweight folding furniture which could be stored away when not in use.

Safety is obviously of paramount importance at this height and even an existing parapet wall might not be high enough for peace of mind. Panels of toughened safety glass may be the solution as they provide the necessary height without the loss of the view, although you might find cleaning the outside of the glass a problem. Slatted timber screens are perhaps more suitable as they allow air to circulate while still maintaining glimpses of the view and, of course, providing a safety barrier. Any proposed alterations to the roofline and the structure will obviously need to be approved by the local authority planning department.

High levels of sunlight and strong winds will cause plants to dry out quickly so a simple irrigation system is essential to avoid constant watering by hand. Choosing the right plants is critical, so look for plants that are best suited to these conditions in their natural habitat. Mediterranean plants and those tolerant of coastal conditions like cistus and lavender are the ones to look for, as well as succulents and grasses such as *Festuca glauca*. A layer of mulch over the planters will also help to conserve moisture. You may find that if your roof terrace is particularly exposed it is more sensible to keep plants below the level of the parapet wall; if, however, conditions are calmer you could grow climbers across strained wires

to create a more intimate setting for dinner parties. Containers can be planted with bulbs and perennials to mark the changing of the seasons, which often slip by unnoticed up among the roof tops. Pots could also be planted with night-scented nicotianas to perfume the air and enhance the atmosphere of a candlelit supper.

ABOVE: The timber pergola across one end of this roof terrace reduces the scale of the whole panoramic view and helps to create a more intimate atmosphere. Straining overhead wires for climbers between two side walls will produce a similar effect.

RIGHT: An unusual setting for a gravel-surfaced terrace among the roof tops. Simple furniture and a few containers are all that is needed, with the drama being provided by the high walls, lean-to conservatory and wide assortment of chimneys.

Ground rules for roof terraces

If you want to create a roof garden it is essential to consult your local planning department first to check whether you can make any structural alterations at all. You should also consult a structural surveyor to advise on the load-bearing capacity of your roof.

*

Plan carefully for safety, wind shelter and drainage.

*

Decking can be a useful surface for roof terraces as it spreads weight evenly over a large surface area. It can also act as a suspended floor if the supporting joists are secured to the side load-bearing walls.

*

Use lightweight containers like fibreglass filled with free-draining compost rather than heavy garden soil.

*

Install a simple irrigation system as pots and planters will dry out quickly. A layer of mulch will also help to conserve moisture.

*

Choose plants suitable for container growing that can tolerate high levels of light and drying winds.

*

Create shelter and safety along the perimeter of the terrace using slatted screens that will not cause wind turbulence nor hide panoramic views.

*

Climbers on a lightweight strained wire will create a simple overhead canopy and make a more intimate setting for dining outside.

*

Install low-level lighting so that you can enjoy the roof garden at night.

ABOVE: Lightweight slats throw striped shade over the deck of this roof garden to make a comfortable area for eating out underneath clear blue skies. Simple irrigation will help to keep plants healthy in environments such as this where high light levels and strong winds will cause plants to dry out quickly.

CONSERVATORIES

ABOVE: The boardwalk forms a bridge over to the raised glass building where timber steps lead down to ground level. The glass roof provides shelter while the woodland setting creates a dappled shade to keep the building cool without the need for blinds.

It may seem slightly tenuous to include conservatories in a book about outdoor living. However, a conservatory is far more than a bolt-on Victorian replica, which is itself really no more than an extension of a house or a sun room with fitted carpets and pot plants. A true conservatory places the emphasis on the growing of plants and forms a strong link between the house and the garden. It can be expensive to build a conservatory and although there are some that you can buy off the peg quite reasonably, a better option may be to choose a custom-made building designed specifically to suit your requirements and your house.

Conservatories are commonly built on to the side of the house that takes the full brunt of the sun, but this is rarely the best position as it can be just too hot for you and your plants, even with blinds and vents. A position on a shadier side of the house may be more comfortable and will also improve the levels of light in the adjacent rooms. Plants that might not survive outside can be grown from ground level or in pots, which can be moved out in warmer seasons. A visit to a botanical garden will show the remarkable tropical environments that can be created under glass, or you may prefer a less steamy Mediterranean version with oleander bushes, vines and citrus trees. Lush-planted conservatories, even with blinds, can be too hot for entertaining

during the day, but on a warm summer's evening they form the perfect setting for a candlelit supper party with friends.

For your comfort and for the survival of your plants, shade and ventilation are essential, as is heating for a constant temperature during the winter. Double glazing will retain heat and help to prevent

too much condensation. Potted plants can be built up in stages to form a dense background of foliage that will link up with the structure of the outdoor shrub planting. Natural stone flooring can also be chosen to match that of a surrounding terrace. It needs to be hardwearing and able to withstand watering and spilt compost, therefore materials like bricks, tiles and flagstones all work well. Furniture that can withstand damp conditions is also best, so cast iron and hardwood work well as do rattan chairs. As a final touch some simple, low-level lighting should be installed to extend the use of your conservatory into the evening and to help create an amicable atmosphere.

ABOVE: On warm summer evenings, the doors of this roof-top conservatory may be left open to let in the night air while the moon and stars shine through the glass roofing, supplementing the artificial lighting and helping to create a magical atmosphere.

SHADE AND SHELTER

ABOVE: Open beams with climbers cast shadows over this high-level terrace to provide a cool and comfortable setting for outdoor entertaining. This type of open beam construction is often more interesting than a solid roof, allowing light to filter through and creating interesting shadow patterns. Here, the vertical pergola supports frame superb views over the distant blue sea.

RIGHT: A beautifully constructed loggia with stone floor allows the owners to enjoy the benefits of indoor and outdoor living. The roof gives protection from rain and the harshest overhead sunlight while the broad openings, with canvas blinds, between the vertical posts let light flood into the room and permit views over the garden.

To enjoy outdoor entertaining fully it is important to be able to sit and eat in comfort protected from the wind, sun and maybe even light showers. Shelter may range from a simple sun umbrella to a roofed veranda or loggia. Alternatively, there is the semi-open beam construction of a pergola, which may be free-standing or, more commonly, set adjoining the house. This will protect interior furnishings from sunlight while creating a link between house and garden.

Pergolas originated in ancient Egypt as supports for vines. Now, however, they have taken on a purely ornamental role, possibly still supporting vines but mainly providing light shade over terraces and other paved areas. The usual construction of posts and open overhead beams is more satisfactory than complete cover, as it allows some light to filter through and interesting patterns can be created by fixing closely spaced timber slats on to the overhead beams. Air can also circulate more freely and climbing roses, wisteria and jasmine will twine around the overhead beams to soften the structure and provide fragrance. A pergola does not normally require planning permission unless you intend to position it on the boundary of your property or if it is to have a covered roof, but it is always worth checking before you begin building. If total protection from the odd shower is required for outdoor dining then a solid-roofed veranda with open sides may be the answer.

The construction of your pergola must be in proportion to the size of the paved area that it shades and it must be compatible with the style of your house. Stained timber beams in a variety of colours can be fun but try to avoid short-lived trends, which may soon look out-of-date. A sturdy construction will be necessary to support heavy climbers like wisteria even if, as a result, the structure may appear too solid and stark while the plants are just starting to grow. It will not help to use thinner sections of timber as these will only buckle in time beneath the weight of the climbing plants. Whatever you do, do not build rustic pergolas, which are extremely flimsy and will not last five minutes.

Careful planning is required to position the pergola so that it covers your dining area adequately, allowing everyone room to move comfortably between the supporting posts. If

to act as viewing panels into the garden. They may be part glazed with stained glass for more interesting tinted views.

Consider how the pergola will look from inside the house, too, making sure that there are no posts in the direct line of doorways and that they are set to either side of windows to allow uninterrupted views into the garden. For a lighter structure, galvanised wires could be strained between two walls or, perhaps, strain wires over a courtyard terrace where space for supporting posts is limited and where a conventional pergola may cut out too much light.

Eating outdoors is a wonderful experience, especially picnics in the dappled shade of birch trees or at a dining table set under the spreading canopy of a eucalyptus tree. But planting trees near the house may prove tricky so you could fit a canvas awning instead. Awnings can easily be fitted to house walls and can be wound out, like those over shop fronts, to provide welcome shade and to prevent the sun from bleaching interior furnishings. They are available in all colours and patterns; plastic-coated canvas is particularly useful, as the colours will not fade.

Translucent fabric can also be draped over pergola beams and tied back to create a tent over your terrace, allowing the light to filter through to create an intimate party atmosphere. Parasols have also grown in popularity over the last few years and staid floral patterns have been replaced with huge sail-like canvases, which look really good on a deck with wooden furniture. Open-sided tents or small marquees are great for dinner parties, informal barbecues or for dancing the night away at a summer party, and all can be either bought or hired.

ABOVE: The pleasure of eating outdoors is an experience not to be missed as long as adequate shelter is provided both for shade from an overbearing sun and from summer showers. If a large shelter is required for a party then it may be preferable to hire a marquee or this ornate tent full of Eastern promise.

OPPOSITE: Awnings can be fitted to house walls and wound out to create shaded sitting areas. Plastic-coated canvas is useful for the awning material as the colours will not fade. In this outdoor room, with the sea in the background, the canvas material has been repeated in the soft furnishings to create a well integrated design.

possible, try to position the posts in areas of planting adjacent to the paving to minimise the risk of people walking into them or, more likely, children running or cycling into them. Remember that posts clothed in climbers will tend to close down the space as well so be sure to allow a bit of extra room between the posts. You will need a minimum height of 2.1m (7ft) from ground level to the underside of the pergola beams, so that even with trailing plants the tallest visitor will be able to walk beneath the canopy comfortably.

Shelter may also be needed at ground level to protect guests from cold winds. Shrub planting, hedges or portable bamboo screens will all help, but leave openings in the planting to maintain views of the surrounding garden. Open timber screens can also be positioned within the planting

LIGHTING

LEFT: Garden lighting has been used here to provide depth and interest around this seating area, where care has been taken not to light up the whole garden with too many glaring lights.

RIGHT: The lighting which has been installed in this garden room creates a wonderful atmosphere for evening dinner parties. Lighting may also be used to link an outdoor room such as this to the house, allowing safe movement from one area to another.

FAR RIGHT: These low-level lights may be positioned among planting to direct visitors to the front door or to highlight pathways around the garden. A lighting designer will be able to offer advice on the most suitable positions and fittings.

The introduction of lighting, both permanent and temporary, will allow you to use your garden in the evening to enjoy outdoor dinner parties and candlelit suppers. Several lights can be used together to provide a comfort zone – their glow should reach out into the landscape, illuminating a broad area to provide a relaxed and friendly feeling around the dining table rather than a wall of darkness. Lighting will also form a strong link between the house and the garden, creating a visual transition from indoors to outdoors and allowing ease of movement from one area to the other.

Lighting designers may be commissioned to give advice on the most suitable light fittings, the best position for lights and the possible effects. They will even give evening demonstrations so that you can see just what you will be getting for your money. Remember, though, that garden lighting should be understated in order to enhance your garden and create depth and interest rather than illuminating the whole scene with glaring lights. With this in mind, try not to get talked into having too many lights by an over-enthusiastic designer.

Great care should be taken, too, with overpowering floodlights which may be all right for security but are far from ideal for atmospheric, ambient lighting and may also be a nuisance to your neighbours. Permanent lighting needs to be subtle and positioned at a low level to provide a soft

background for planting. Small spotlights can be introduced and carefully angled to highlight a particular plant, a statue or another focal point but the beam of light needs to be aimed away from dining areas to avoid dazzling guests. Low-level lights can also be positioned to direct visitors to the front door and then again out into the garden and on to the terrace. Porch lights are best positioned to one side, not directly above head height, as lights can attract unwelcome flying insects. Great care must also be taken when siting lights to illuminate steps. If these are wrongly positioned the steps can be thrown into shadow and become quite dangerous.

Simple low-level and low-voltage lighting is all that is needed to set a wonderful scene for a party and provide drama with dancing shadows and silhouettes or

115

ABOVE: Temporary lighting makes an interesting addition to more permanent lighting for special occasions such as barbecues and supper parties. Garden flares on spikes in the lawn can be quite dramatic or you may choose these simple candles set into coloured glass tubes, which can be placed among planting and will provide a more gentle light.

illuminated reflections in a still pool. Night lights may be positioned to uplight, down-light and even provide light from the side to create fascinating effects and a magical atmosphere. Coloured lights can also be used but with great restraint, as they may give off a sickly hue and result in a scene similar to a fairy grotto. It is probably best to stick with white light, which will enhance the natural colours within your garden.

Uplighters can be used for an effect known as 'grazing', a technique that angles light across a textured wall, throwing its surface into strong relief and silhouetting adjacent plants. 'Moonlighting', as the term suggests, is a technique that mimics the effect of the light of the moon by setting lights high up in a tree to give off a soft glow on the plants down below, adding depth to the garden as well as providing some security. 'Shadowing' is the wonderful effect produced by aiming a light at a plant with architectural foliage to cast fascinating shadows on the wall behind.

Lighting can, of course, be used to stunning effect in association with water. There is the obvious need to highlight pools in patio areas for safety but, in addition to this, it can be breathtaking to see the elevation of the house illuminated and reflected in an adjacent pool. Waterfalls and fountains that are lit from below also look magical as long as the lights are carefully positioned so as not to highlight otherwise hidden pipes and

cables. Fibre optic lights are particularly useful in this context as light is produced from a single source and reflected through strands of glass fibre, ending in hundreds of sparkling points of light. No electricity runs through the strands, making them safe to drape through waterfalls where the glinting light looks fantastic.

Ultimately, it is the effect of the light that is important and not the light fitting. There are some fairly ugly imitation lamps and lanterns on the market and while it is important to be able to reach lights for maintenance you really do not want your attention to be drawn to them. Light fittings work best if they are simple, streamlined and small enough to be set inconspicuously among low planting. There are many lights that now fit these criteria, which are manufactured in weatherproof stainless steel, brass, copper and cast aluminium.

In addition to permanent lighting you can also introduce temporary lighting to add to the special atmosphere of eating outdoors. Electric lights can again be used but on a string of low-voltage spiked fittings, which you can move around yourself and fix in the most suitable position close to the patio. You could also hang a simple string of white lights from the pergola or the branches of a tree, and add to the party atmosphere by setting each hanging light in a coloured paper lantern. Of course, electricity is not the only source of light for eating and sitting areas: I sometimes sit outside late in the evening by the glow of a simple gas lamp.

Garden flares stuck into the lawn will produce a dramatic effect for informal parties while candles are gentler and more romantic. Candles are best set into glass

FAR LEFT: There is a wide variety of candle holders and lanterns on the market which can easily be positioned around the garden to give a warm glow.

LEFT: The pale glow of candle light illuminates the pretty heart-shaped pot holders which secure the lights to the tree.

FAR LEFT: An ornate lantern, placed here on a low pillar amongst waterside planting, spreads a soft light over the water's edge.

LEFT: The individual pumpkin lights, grouped here in a tray, may be used to line a path or driveway to welcome your guests to a party and show them the way.

Lighting can certainly add a great sense of drama; here, simple storm lanterns have been positioned to illuminate this fabulous setting and create a magical atmosphere under the clear night sky. Storm lanterns are safer than an open flame, especially here near a tent or awning. A lantern will also prevent the candle from being blown over but do be aware that the lamp itself may become hot. When setting up lighting for an evening party, it is often a good idea to add a few citronella candles to the table decorations as these will help keep mosquitoes away.

ABOVE: Candles may be set into a variety of glass bowls and jars which will prevent the flame from being blown out and stop wax dripping on to the table. The candle can be positioned in sand in the bottom of the jar which will also help keep the container stable.

bowls so that they do not blow out in the breeze and to prevent wax from being blown on to the table. They can also be placed in ornamental storm lanterns and steel ship's lanterns that can be painted with enamel paint or decorated with punch holes. Another inexpensive idea for a party is to place candles in brown paper bags weighted down with sand – dotted around the garden or lining paths they produce an ethereal glow. The occasional citronella candle on the table will help to keep the mosquitoes away, and it goes without saying that great care should be taken with all light fittings and candles, especially if there are young children around.

Safely lit

Use a qualified electrician for all electrical installations.

*

Plan lighting circuits at the same time as the rest of the garden, not as an afterthought.

*

Route cable trenches along the foot of boundaries or the edges of a lawn and avoid running them through areas of regular cultivation. Draw and keep a simple diagram showing the route of the cable runs.

*

Bury electrical cables to a minimum depth of 45cm (18in) and lay them through a protective sheath as an extra precaution.

*

Take advice from a lighting designer on fittings and make sure that any fittings and cabling you purchase are armoured and suitable for garden use.

*

Fit a circuit breaker on the end of a cable run to cut off the power if the cable is damaged.

*

Place all exterior plug sockets and connections in waterproof housings.

*

Locate switches for outdoor lighting within the house if possible.

*

When using candles or flares be aware of the dangers of an open flame, especially near clothing, awnings and garden tents. If candles are placed in bowls or lanterns remember that these will become very hot.

*

Site flares in open spaces and do not use them if there are young children around.

*

Have a source of cold water or a bucket of sand close to hand in case of any accident.

COOKING AND EATING

There really is something special about cooking and eating out of doors, particularly if you are lucky enough to live by the sea and can enjoy beach barbecues or if your garden has a copse of trees where you can picnic in a woodland clearing for the real outdoor effect.

If you live in a country where the climate is hot and dry for much of the year then you may consider a small outdoor kitchen with cooker, sink, storage cupboards and work surfaces. For most of us, however, outdoor cooking will not extend as far as this but it will almost certainly include a barbecue. Cooking at a barbecue tends to become the focal point of any gathering so be sure to allow plenty of room so that small groups of people can congregate easily.

Barbecues range from the small, instant varieties that can only be used once and are then thrown away, to the larger gas portables with hotplates and a rotisserie. There are certainly a huge number of sophisticated models on the market, but unless you are a regular entertainer of a large number of people then you may be better off with something more modest, which will present less of a storage problem, too.

If you enjoy barbecuing, you may wish to build your own, which will certainly take care of the storage problem. The ideal site is close to the kitchen and the patio where food is prepared and people gather to talk and eat. These structures can be temporary

ABOVE AND RIGHT:
Outdoor meals can really be quite special, whether it is just a lunchtime snack for one of the children or a long leisurely supper with family and friends. Everything seems so much more relaxed outside and it really does not matter about spilt drinks or crumbs.

Barbecue tips

Keep a close eye on children around the barbecue and watch out for flying sparks.

*

Use special barbecue firelighters that are safe and do not taint the food.

*

Brush cooking oil on the grill before cooking to prevent the food from sticking.

*

A spray bottle of water is useful to douse any flames that shoot up from burning fat. When you have finished cooking you can always tip water over the coals to preserve them for next time; beware of the hot steam, though.

*

Cooking in your best white shirt is not a good idea. If you are dressed for the party always wear an apron over your clothes.

*

Growing herbs nearby can be useful, allowing you to pick the occasional sprig of rosemary to throw on to the coals for fragrance or to decorate the table.

*

Eating barbecues can be a messy business for your guests so provide lots of good quality paper napkins and place several finger bowls on the table, too.

ABOVE: If you are a regular barbecue cook you may enjoy using a sophisticated gas barbecue with a rotisserie and hotplates, but do allow plenty of room close by as it will be sure to become the focal point of any gathering.

ABOVE RIGHT: If you are an occasional outdoor cook then a modest portable stove would be ideal. This type of barbecue is also suitable for taking on holiday for use down on the beach.

– a construction of dry-laid bricks over which a grill is laid, and the whole thing can then be dismantled after the party. Alternatively, they may be more permanent structures with built-in seats and storage cupboards. As usual, it is the simplest designs that work best and sit most comfortably in the landscape; large, ostentatious affairs with a brick, stone or tiled chimney are best avoided.

Brick barbecues should be built at a comfortable working height of about 75–85cm (2ft 6in–2ft 10in) or at about 45cm (18in) if you prefer to sit down while cooking. When I use my barbecue I simply remove a dry slab which covers the top of it and then sit down to cook. When we have finished and the coals have cooled, the slab is replaced and the structure is once more a low stone bench, which passes almost unnoticed among the surrounding shrubs. Barbecues do not have to be a summertime luxury; cooking hot dogs and burgers on a cold, starlit evening, perhaps on Bonfire Night, can be great fun if you all wrap up warm and I have even roasted chestnuts in the glowing coals at Christmas. The hardy barbecue cook should always have a parasol close by in case of a sudden downpour.

If you like to cook a variety of things outside, from a loaf of bread to the Sunday roast, then you could consider a terracotta beehive oven, which cooks food by radiant heat without drying it out. The terracotta oven will need to be covered and protected from frost damage and it will also need thoughtful siting in order to avoid becoming an eyesore when not in use.

If you are barbecuing for a large party you may need to hire a commercial-sized barbecue and possibly catering staff to help

LEFT: Outdoor cooking for most of us is limited to a small barbecue. However, if your climate is suitable you may benefit from an outdoor kitchen with a sink and work surfaces as well as a stove.

ABOVE: Having an outside sink is ideal for washing and preparing food and also allows everyone to wash and clean up before a meal without traipsing through the house.

ABOVE: Verandas and loggias are obviously ideal outdoor rooms for entertaining as there is no need to worry about a sudden downpour ruining the party.

ABOVE RIGHT: Having everything ready and planned is essential before you start to cook, especially if the barbecue is at some distance from the house.

out as well. For a small group of friends the whole operation is on a much smaller scale but, even so, I will often use a portable barbecue in addition to the brick-built one to ensure that the cooking area is large enough to cope with all the food. You need to start the fire about three-quarters of an hour before you are ready to start cooking, by which time the coals should have turned to a white ash colour. Spread the hot coals out evenly beneath the grill to ensure that everything is cooked at the same time. I usually put the empty grill over the fire first

in order to burn off any residue, which saves on dirty washing up.

Make sure that everything is ready before you start cooking, including sauces for basting – there is a vast array of ready-made sauces and marinades available in all supermarkets in addition to your own home-made favourites. Use good quality meats including pork, lamb, chicken drumsticks and herb sausages, but avoid meat with too much fat on it or you will end up with an inferno as the fat melts on to the charcoal. Chunks of corn on the cob, basted with seasoned olive oil, are so tasty and really easy to cook as are salmon fillets marinated in rosemary and garlic. Oily fish is best for barbecuing and it will not fall apart if you cook it for long enough to firm it up on one side before turning it over. Burgers are very quick to cook, and marinated lamb, pork or chicken kebabs skewered with onions and red pepper are delicious served up with a crisp salad, garlic bread and an ice-cold bottle of beer.

A picnic lunch on a rug under a tree or at the end of the garden as the sun is setting can be great fun as spilt drinks and crumbs are really no problem at all. The only 'furni-ture' needed is a rug; drinks and food can be kept in a cool box and there is probably no need for cutlery or glasses, just plastic cups and plates. Picnics in the garden should be very relaxed occasions, there is

BELOW: Preparing to cook outside will not only include having all the right knives, tongs and skewers but also a selection of sauces and marinades, many of which may be ready made in addition to your own home made varieties.

RIGHT: A good location will always add to the pleasure of an outdoor meal whether it is a picnic by the riverside, a beach barbecue or as here in the sunlight under a vine overlooking a wooded valley.

no point turning it into a banquet otherwise you will end up carting food in and out of the house after each course. Everything should be easy to eat without knives and forks, like rolls, cold pieces of pie, crudités and dips, fresh fruit and thick slices of cake. All of these can be stored and carried easily in a hamper or cool box, and the only time you may need to cheat a little is by keeping trifles, ice creams and other puddings in the refrigerator and freezer until you are ready to eat them.

Like barbecues, picnics do not need hot weather to be enjoyable. On a crisp autumn day, a party of friends returning to your garden with healthy appetites after a long walk will soon devour cups of steaming soup with crusty bread, spicy chorizo and bowls of warming chilli con carne.

FURNITURE

LEFT: Hardwood furniture is available today in a wide range of styles, including this traditional steamer which looks just right set on a timber deck against a weather board house. Hardwood benches can be left out all year although folding seats such as this would be best stored under cover.

OPPOSITE: Eating outdoors may mean a picnic on a rug under a tree or lunch in the cool comfort of a garden room. Here, sunlight filters through the slatted roof on to sturdy furniture on a warm tiled floor. Raised planters and potted plants bring the garden into the room.

ABOVE: A lot of portable furniture can be overpriced and unattractive or uncomfortable, unlike the classic deckchair which is extremely comfortable and manages to look good just about everywhere.

RIGHT: The chairs may be portable but the table is definitely permanent, remaining in this cool outdoor room for family meals and supper parties. The built-in bench at the far end serves as an additional seat and a planting shelf.

Permanent furniture can be planned in at an early stage of the garden design. By incorporating benches and seats in the structure of the patio or the terrace you can save space and eliminate the need for portable furniture and the additional storage that is required. The seats may be built to form eye-catching focal points and will provide an ideal place for picnics as well as for relaxation. Benches can be tied in with barbecues and raised beds or low retaining walls. In fact, any change of level, even steps, can make good impromptu seating for informal parties.

If you plan to build your own seating, whether around a tree or adjacent to a barbecue, the right height is about 45cm (18in) above the ground. Slatted timber is warmer and more comfortable than stone but you could always use cushions as well. Very often a stone or teak garden seat is so heavy that although in theory it is portable, in practice it is too heavy to move around and could therefore be considered a permanent fixture. Furniture such as this, which will remain in the garden throughout the years, must have a timeless quality. It should be positioned against a backdrop of shrubs or hedging or underneath a tree, where it will both look good and enjoy good views. Picnic tables are another heavy item that will tend to remain in a fixed position. Sometimes no more than a perch is needed for a brief rest and here logs or well positioned boulders around a woodland glade make ideal informal seats.

Portable garden furniture has really improved over recent years with beautiful designs that easily compare with interior styles. Furniture should be in keeping with its setting, even if it is not on view all year, as it is the furnishings in a garden that provide the finishing touches to the design. While some furniture is terribly over-designed and over-priced, lacking both aesthetic appeal and comfort, there are

ABOVE: The blue-painted chair has been positioned in the perfect place to enjoy the sun, surrounded by flowers and the fragrance of the climbing rose; the colours in the garden tone beautifully with those of the house.

RIGHT: Some home-made furniture can look awful, but not this charming little table which has been constructed on the top of an old tree trunk and makes a wonderful perch for pot plants or a glass of wine.

other affordable styles like the classic deckchair that look good in any setting and are extremely comfortable. Try out furniture before buying it as comfort is all-important and check measurements, too, so as to make sure that the proportions are right for your patio and that the furniture will actually fit.

There is a superb range of hardwood garden furniture available. These benches, seats and tables can be left out all year

LEFT: The furniture in this garden has been laid out for relaxed entertaining with the low stone walls constructed at just the right height for a seat and large cushions to provide extra comfort.

RIGHT: This well constructed, rustic-style bench looks perfect in its position on this sunny timber deck.

round, although they may need to be treated once in a while with teak oil to preserve the natural colour of the wood. Folding chairs in the same material are fine but not as sturdy. And, as with all hardwoods, you should always check that the timber originated in sustainable forests.

Metal furniture is available as heavy cast tables and chairs, which are barely portable, or as lighter wrought iron that needs paint-ing to maintain its condition. Aluminium or plastic-coated steel are both lighter and easier to maintain. There are also a lot of chairs in great contemporary designs, which combine wooden slats with metal frames and are both lightweight and easy to stack or fold away. Be wary, though, when these chairs are marketed 'for occasional outdoor use', as they will sit on the patio rusting after the slightest hint of rain, exposing what you thought was an economical purchase as in fact a waste of money. Plastic or lacquered resin chairs are lightweight and only need wiping clean, but they can present a problem in windy sites where they will be easily blown over.

Wooden steamer chairs with curved wooden slats, which fit the contours of the body, are often both beautiful to look at and comfortable to recline on. Simple canvas chairs often get the best reviews for style and comfort and even the humble deckchair has seen a new lease of life with a built-in foot rest and canopy.

Cushions will always improve comfort and are suitable for all furniture styles, forming a visual link with awnings, para-sols and even interior furnishings. Picnic rugs on the lawn can have waterproof backs or simply be made from cotton which, unlike some woollen rugs, can be cleaned in the washing machine.

Numerous magazines now sell or review different types of outdoor furniture, which can prove extremely useful. Read the reports carefully, and find out where the furniture can be seen and tried out before buying as it is generally too risky to buy straight from a magazine without testing for comfort. The reviewers often describe the more elegant steel furniture as 'ideal for a quick coffee', which probably means you will be uncomfortable after ten minutes.

Whatever style of furniture you decide to choose, remember to consider the purpose you want it to fulfil before buying – do you want a chair for dining at a table or just for general lounging? When you make your choice, you also need to consider storage needs. Furniture that can be left outside all year may be more practical. Most garages never have enough storage space and summerhouses are too expensive to end up as sheds. Equally, you do not want to end up buying an unattractive shed for the sole purpose of storing chairs.

GARDEN PARTIES

Organising outdoor parties is a serious business, which is why there are so many companies that will do it all for you. Even a small barbecue party can be hard work, so when guest numbers are approaching thirty it is probably time to enlist some help. Whether you are planning the party yourself or calling in the professionals it is always fun to liven up the event up by introducing a theme.

Fancy dress always breaks the ice – why not have a Wild West barbecue or a Mad Hatter's tea party, perhaps substituting something more interesting for the tea? Sixties parties can give you the chance to play some great music while a Seventies theme with platform soles and retro clothes and hairdos cannot possibly be boring. A Horror party with chains hanging from the marquee and candles burning in red-painted jars along with games of murder in the dark is always eventful, and if everyone is still around in the morning you can start all over again with a breakfast party!

If you do plan a party at home involving a marquee an area of lawn is essential, as these cannot be fixed to a paved surface. Small garden tents with steel frames and open sides can be hired for most garden parties, to provide shade and keep the rain off while creating a more intimate party atmosphere. Large marquees of about 18m (60ft) by 9m (30ft) can also be hired, fully lined and fitted with doors and a dance floor.

ABOVE AND RIGHT:
A large-scale party does require a fair amount of organisation and help commandeered from family and friends, no matter how young. You certainly cannot hope to do everything yourself and still enjoy the party, so it may even be wise to hand everything over to a professional party organiser.

Plants, lighting, cushions and furniture are all extras that can also be hired. There is nothing to prevent you having an outdoor party at any time of the year, as heaters can be installed in a marquee in winter or side canopies can be raised in summer to allow for better air circulation. A marquee can usually be hired by the day or for a weekend and the hire company should erect it and take it down for you – just make sure that your lawn is large enough and that there is sufficient space at the sides for guy ropes. (There are some models that do not actually need guy ropes.) Themed marquees are also available; I have come across a company that has superb Bedouin-style tents, ideal for an Arabian Nights party, which look stunning decked out with wonderful carpets, rugs and cushions, palm trees and Ali-baba baskets. Burning incense and a giant hookah pipe for decoration all add to the ambience.

ABOVE LEFT: It is often the small details which make a successful party and that may include a few of your own home-made delicacies to provide the finishing touch.

ABOVE: Barbecue parties are always popular but do remember that not everyone eats meat so try fish as well, choosing oily fish which tends not to fall apart.

131

If you are considering a party, a lot of planning and list writing will have to be done. You cannot hope to do everything yourself for a large-scale celebration – if you try to you will be too exhausted to enjoy the party at the end, so enlist help from your family and maybe ask for a hand with the cooking. Buy some ready-prepared food if you have a specialist delicatessen or good, reliable butcher in your area, but be wary of some mass-produced supermarket offerings and never buy food for a party without trying it yourselves at home first. You will definitely need plenty of refrigerator space so accept all offers of help, and if you plan to serve hot food then you will need hot plates as well. Practically everything you will need can be hired and you will probably be wise to hire crockery and cutlery so that you have enough for everyone, and so that it all matches. Another brilliant advantage of hiring crockery, glasses and cutlery is that most hirers will take it back unwashed for a small extra fee – in my experience this is money very well spent.

Flowers look lovely for outdoor as well as indoor dinner parties but stick to simple arrangements, which are low enough on the table so that you can see everyone sitting opposite you without peering round leaves. Candles protected from the breeze in small glass bowls add the finishing touch to a dinner table and, undoubtedly, to the atmosphere of a successful party.

Children's parties often need more planning and direction as young children are not very good at impromptu, unorganised parties which can soon get out of hand, bringing out the worst in them. Children need to be kept safe and amused, as well as organised, so hiring an entertainer, magi-

LEFT: The beauty of enlisting professional help is that they will carry stocks of everything you need, from all the furniture and large quantities of matching crockery and cutlery to tablecloths and candelabra. RIGHT: If you can be sure of a spell of good weather then a party on the lawn is terrific, although it may be wise to have a small marquee as a contingency for bad weather and also as a place for children to play in the shade.

cian or face-painter will all help. Make sure you know the exact length of time the entertainer will be keeping the children amused and then fill in the rest of the time with lots of different games – some boisterous and some sitting down. Finally, always make sure that you have twice as many games organised as you think you will need.

A small marquee or garden tent is also a good idea for children's parties to keep them in the shade or out of the rain and the mud. Some of these tents are fitted over the top of a large paddling pool, which is great fun but obviously requires extra supervision. A giant tepee could be hired and all the children could dress up as cowboys and Indians, or you could consider numerous other themes: pirates, fairies,

superheroes, Flintstones, Teddy Bears' Picnic, spacemen, vampires, a beach party, and so on. Pirate parties are always fun, as well as easy, because everyone can wear ragged trousers, a striped T-shirt and spotted scarf, just right for swashbuckling sword fights in the garden and a treasure hunt. Lines of bunting easily made from coloured triangles of paper, glued on to string and stretched over the lawn, will add to the nautical party theme, with a Jolly Roger in there, too.

When it is time to go home, handing out party bags should help to speed up the departure of those reluctant to leave; nothing elaborate is needed – just a plain bag simply decorated, containing a piece of cake and a few inexpensive goodies will do.

PAPER LANTERNS

ABOVE RIGHT: A simple string of lights hanging from the roof beams or pergola will enhance the party mood and add a special atmosphere to outdoor entertaining.

BELOW: These colourful paper lanterns produce a warm glow and can be decorated to suit the theme of your party.

These simple paper lanterns are easy to make and when strung up as a garland of coloured lights they will add something special to the wonderful atmosphere of an outdoor party. The width of the lantern will be governed by the diameter of the lampholder, although the length of the lanterns can be varied for added interest. Pictures made from different-coloured paper which are stuck on to the sides of each lantern may show a simple shape such as the moon, or it could be a design perhaps of a Christmas tree which relates to the theme of the party.

MATERIALS
* Large piece of coloured paper, minimum size A3
* Smaller sheets of coloured paper for patterns
* Two thin strips of wood each totalling 42cm (16in)
* PVA glue
* Clear sticky tape
* Lampholder and clips or strong wire

TOOLS
* Pencil
* Ruler
* Scissors

LEFT: Lighting such as this pumpkin can be used to complement more permanent lighting on special occasions. Temporary lights are extremely useful for positioning around the garden perhaps to illuminate a wider area of lawn than usual for a large party or to highlight paths and driveways. Most lights like these are fairly simple and inexpensive but great care must always be taken with their positioning because of the obvious danger of a naked flame.

1 Mark three pencil lines across the width of the coloured paper at equal spacings, the same distance apart as the diameter of your lampholder, to form the four sides of the lantern. Cut out two designs from paper of a different colour and stick them on to two sides on the outside of the lantern so that when the lantern is complete, the two designs are on opposite sides.

2 Form sharp creases in the lantern paper along the pencil lines so that the paper can be folded into a crisp, neat shape. Take two strips of wood which are equal in length to the coloured paper that forms the lantern. Cut each strip of wood into four equal pieces, each of which will be the same length as one side of the lantern and thus the same length as the diameter of your lampholder.

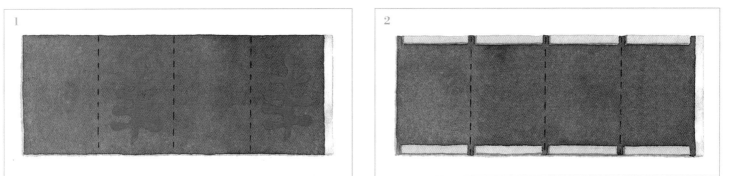

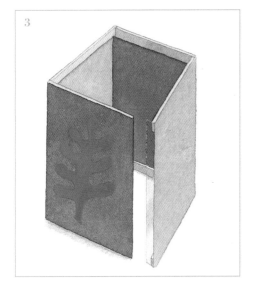

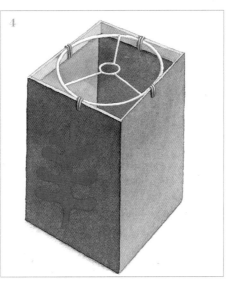

Stick one piece of wood to the inside top and bottom of each side panel of the lantern ensuring, as you work, that you can form the 90 degree angle at each corner for the finished lantern. These pieces of wood give strength to the lantern, holding it in shape and forming a firm fixing point for the lampholder.

3 Attach a length of clear sticky tape along the edge of one end of the paper and stick it to the inside edge of the other end to form the lantern.

4 Position the lampholder at the top of the lantern and carefully push it into place. Use clips or strong wire wound around the strips of wood to hold it firmly in place.

BARBECUE

ABOVE: There are plenty of elaborate recipes and marinades which can be used for barbecued food, but it takes a lot to beat sausages and ketchup which are always a success with young children.

Many brick-built barbecues look obtrusive and sit uncomfortably in a well-designed garden. This low-level barbecue, however, softened by shrubs, doubles up as a seat and provides an attractive addition. It is a simple brick box construction 45cm (18in) high, built in stretcher bond brickwork laid on a concrete footing. The paved top is formed from 45cm x 45cm (18in x 18in) paving slabs, to match the patio, one of which is laid dry and can easily be removed in order to use the barbecue.

Flat steel bars are bedded into the brickwork to support the barbecue grill at different levels above the coals. Simple handles may be bought to hold the grill, slide it out and lift it into the new position. The lowest-level bars can be used to hold a tray for charcoal but the one in our barbecue, which is pictured above, burnt through years ago so now I simply burn the coals on the concrete base and this seems to work just as well and doesn't affect the food.

TOP: Some large, built-in barbecues can look quite obtrusive while this low-level brick barbecue, softened by planting, sits comfortably in the garden and doubles up as a bench with a paved top to match the patio.

RIGHT: Sausages and burgers do not have to be treats just for sunny days alone; cooking hot dogs under starlit skies, perhaps at a bonfire party, can be good fun, too, where everyone can wrap up in warm clothes and huddle around the fire.

MATERIALS
* Concrete
* 150 well-fired and frostproof bricks
* Mortar, about one barrowful
* 12 brick butterfly ties
* 10 flat steel bars, 38cm x 5cm x 0.6cm (15in x 2in x ⅛in)
* 5 pre-cast concrete paving slabs, 45cm x 45cm (18 x 18in)

TOOLS
* Tape measure
* Spade
* Shovel
* Wheelbarrow
* Brick trowel
* String line
* Spirit level
* Club hammer
* Brick bolster
* Timber straight edge
* Short pipe or bucket handle for finishing joints
* Steel float

1 Roughly mark out the area for the barbecue and seat, excavate and cart away the soil. The area should be dug out to allow for a 15cm (6in) depth of concrete which should finish about 5cm (2in) below ground level. Lay the concrete to cover an area 7.5cm (3in) wider all round the outline of the brick walls. This outline can then be marked out on the surface of the concrete so that you can lay your first course of bricks. Note that you will have to cut bricks at each end of the barbecue/seat so that when the top slabs are laid they overhang the side brick walls by a small amount. You will also have to cut the bricks at either side of the barbecue itself and tie them in with brick ties. Build up the corners of the brickwork first, checking constantly with a spirit level to ensure that the walls are vertical and the bricks are level. Then you can fill in the brickwork between the corners, using a straight edge, spanning from one corner to another, to tap the bricks down to a level finish. Rub the mortar joints between the bricks smooth with a bucket handle or short length of pipe.

2 Use strong mortar or concrete to fill the base area and smooth it off with a steel float. Push flat steel bars into the mortar joints on every course, either side of the barbecue, which will support a cooking grill at different heights.

3 When you have laid the sixth or top course of brickwork, then lay two flat steel bars in the position as shown. These bars will allow you to form the mortar joints between the seating slabs without the mortar falling down into the cavity. Lay four paving slabs on mortar to finish level and in line with each other, with a slight overhang all around the brick walls. Spread mortar and bring it to a smooth flat finish on the brick lip around the barbecue. Allow it to dry and set hard so that when a slab is laid on it, that slab will finish at the same level as the others. You will need to get a grill made to slide into position and a charcoal tray if you prefer.

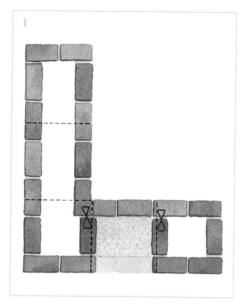

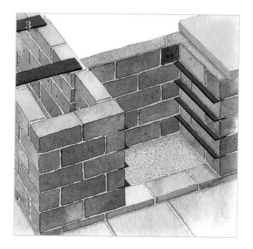

ABOVE: Sausages are the perennial favourite, but try to avoid those that are too fatty as the melted fat will drop on to the coals, sending flames up to blacken the food. Good quality pork and lamb are very tasty and so are chicken drumsticks. Corn on the cob is very easy to cook, together with vegetable kebabs made up of courgettes, red peppers and onions.

HERBS IN A STRAWBERRY POT

Strawberry pots are brilliant for growing herbs, as well as strawberries, or you could combine the two for a stunning display that is both ornamental and productive. The pots are easy to plant up and the tower of foliage looks very effective – a range of pots set up in this way on the patio close to the kitchen is ideal for nipping outside to pick a few fresh herbs when cooking. Growing herbs in this way is especially useful if space is limited as, perhaps, in a small town courtyard garden or roof terrace. The sides of the pot may be planted up with low growing and carpeting plants such as thyme and marjoram while more upright herbs such as the purple-leafed sage or chives should be planted in the top. If you do want to grow strawberries as well, choose the delicious alpine strawberry, as it is not such a vigorous plant and feed it regularly with liquid tomato feed from flowering until all the fruit are picked. You will need to keep the pot well watered, as the compost around the planting holes will tend to dry out.

MATERIALS
* Terracotta strawberry pot
* Pieces of broken terracotta crocks
* Small bag of multipurpose potting compost
* Selection of herbs and alpine strawberries

TOOLS
* Garden trowel
* Watering can
* Old newspaper

TOP: Herbs really do give such tremendous value as they are cheap and easy to grow, they are fragrant and can be used in cooking, too.

LEFT: Growing herbs in a container is wise for invasive plants such as mint and useful for small gardens with limited growing space.

OPPOSITE: The combination of strawberries and herbs in a terracotta pot looks superb and is productive as well. Using a strawberry pot allows you to plant alpine strawberries or low-growing herbs such as thyme and marjoram through the holes in the side, while sage and other taller herbs may be grown in the top.

1 Place the strawberry pot on newspaper on a firm, dry, paved surface. The hole in the base of the pot should be covered with broken crocks which will allow drainage while preventing the soil from being washed out.

2 With a garden trowel, fill the pot with compost to about 2.5cm (1in) below the lowest row of planting pockets in the side of the pot. Any spilt compost can be tipped off the newspaper and re-used in other pots.

3 After first removing their pots, start to plant the small herbs or strawberry plants through the lowest side planting holes. With very small plants you can plant from the outside, but if they are too big for this then place the plant inside the pot and carefully push the foliage through to the outside. Backfill compost around the rootballs of the plants to hold them firm and then add more compost to just below the next row of planting pockets.

4 Once all the side pockets have been planted then the more upright herbs can be planted in the top of the pot. These plants should be well firmed in and the compost should be brought right up to the base of the lip at the top of the pot. Place the pot where you want it to stand and then water it carefully so that the water does not run out of the planting holes.

kathryn ireland, **summers in france**

In the south of France, not far from Toulouse in the Tarn-et-Garonne region, lies the summer retreat of Kathryn Ireland where she comes to escape from the hustle and bustle of California. The house is a nineteenth-century farmhouse, typical of the area, with large rooms and high ceilings simply decorated in a mix of minimalist and French country. Like the house, the garden is simple and rugged, too; there are four acres of lawn around the house and large oak, ash and beech trees close by which in winter reveal stunning views towards the Pyrenees.

Kathryn grew up in England but now lives and works for nine months of the year in California, where she runs her successful interior design business with such illustrious clients as Steve Martin, Meg Ryan and Anjelica Huston.

ABOVE: Local produce adds to the enjoyment of lunch and supper parties at Kathryn Ireland's French home, where fresh herbs and vegetables can be picked from the kitchen garden.

LEFT: The old hay barn at the end of the house is the venue for most meals. Candelabra, flares and the glowing barbecue add to the atmosphere of this impressive room.

RIGHT: Guests from Hollywood, New York and London fly in during the summer to stay at the farmhouse and enjoy the long candlelit dinners which seem to last forever.

About ten years ago Kathryn came to France with her former husband, Gary Weis, and spent some time driving around the French countryside looking for a suitable property to buy. As a child Kathryn had been taken on grand tours of France and Italy by her parents, and she felt that a grounding in European culture would also be useful for her own children. Kathryn and Gary have three boys, Oscar, Otis and Louis, who spend the first month of their summer in France at the local school which is proving to be the best way for them to learn the language. Their time in France also gives them a break from Nintendo, baseball and Tinseltown and a chance to enjoy more pastoral activities such as collecting milk, picking fruit from the orchards and horse riding.

When Kathryn first found the property ten years ago she immediately fell in love with it; the views were wonderful and the rolling landscape evoked fond memories of England's West Country.

She was not even aware of the rusting old cars and heaps of broken machinery which littered the garden – nor that the purchase of the house and 20 hectares (50 acres) of land included a working vineyard producing more than 10,000 bottles of wine a year!

Over the years Kathryn has developed the garden, keeping it very much in character with the area. Most of the work has been involved in clearing the ground of all the broken machinery and installing a swimming pool with traditional mosaics around the edges. She cut up old wine barrels to make plant containers which are now filled with geraniums and lavender. A herb and kitchen garden were also created as well as an orchard. Kathryn also found that roses had been planted at the end of each row of vines, so every year she plants more and more roses to go with them. In addition to the fields of sunflowers which appear to be part of the garden, Kathryn would sometime like to grow a field of lavender as well.

The hammock is the favourite place to rest for both children and adults as it has been positioned to command great views across the valley.

Seats and benches are arranged under the canopy of overhanging branches which provide shade on the south side of the house.

Throughout the summer, the garden is well used, particularly the swimming pool and the gravel terrace to the south of the house where family and friends play boules and enjoy many barbecues. There are comfortable chairs and benches set out in the shade of the large trees and a hammock, which everyone loves, positioned to give good views over a valley. The garden has a great atmosphere with large lawns, haystacks and outbuildings where the children play, and there is also a treehouse with swings and rope ladders which Kathryn's brother, Robert, built in one of the huge trees. Another of the children's favourite pastimes is searching for hidden artefacts throughout the 20 hectares (50 acres) farm with a metal detector. The simplicity and rural charm of her French house have proved to be the ideal antidote to Kathryn's busy life in Los Angeles and the perfect place to entertain friends, who fly in from London and Hollywood to enjoy long candlelit dinners in the old barn.

Ground rules

* Keep the garden in character with the property and surrounding landscape.

* Avoid fussiness and allow children to play unrestricted.

* There is never any excuse for litter, even in a rambling farmhouse garden.

* Everyone must share the workload of watering, weeding and picking fruit.

Barbecues and boules are two of the regular activities which take place on the long gravel terrace next to the house.

It is a really great place for children to play with huge lawns, haystacks and a treehouse complete with rope ladder and swing.

the bournes, **an island paradise**

Some three-and-a-half years ago, Clive and Joy Bourne began work on their winter home on the island of Nevis in the West Indies, bought as a place to which to escape from the bleak British winters where they could entertain their friends in tropical sunshine. Initially, their land which lies in the Jones Bay area of the island was covered with impenetrable vegetation, but its beachside proximity and breathtaking views made it an ideal location for the colonial/Caribbean style house which now stands there.

Two guest houses were also built in the same style to accommodate the Bourne's friends in comfort. The gardens which surround the buildings are magnificent; a cobbled drive sweeps up to the front of the house between lines of palm trees and oleander bushes, lawns of Bermuda grass flow down to the beach and heliconias line the veranda overlooking the swimming pool terrace. The Bournes have now enjoyed two Christmases relaxing with their friends around the pool in their island garden, but they knew at the outset that achieving this idyllic garden would be fraught with difficulties – they were not wrong! To help them create this paradise garden they enlisted the professional expertise of the English garden designer, Julie Toll.

ABOVE: Entertaining on the pool terrace surrounded by exotic plants is a way of life at the Bourne's home on the tropical island of Nevis.

LEFT: Showy plants like bougainvillea, ginger and heliconias all flourish in the garden and look wonderful when used as cut flowers for the house or for decorating the veranda.

RIGHT Dinner parties are often held on the veranda, which commands a stunning panoramic view over the sea towards the island of St. Kitts.

Julie prepared a design for the garden and was then asked to manage the implementation of the scheme, working closely with the architect of the house and her own contract manager.

Building a garden in England may sometimes involve a few difficulties although with experienced contractors, good material suppliers and favourable weather conditions the problems tend to be minimal. On a tropical island with no trained labour or tools or equipment and the occasional plague of insects which can destroy vegetation in a couple of weeks, it can be a different experience altogether. Not to mention the hurricane season from June to October, when storms can destroy vast areas of landscape.

Machinery and chemical sprays were imported from the United States as well as the plants, which came from Florida. Hand tools were brought in from the United Kingdom along with spare parts, as repair skills on the island are low or non-existent.

A belt of mangroves along one border of the property is a haven for wildlife and helps shelter the house and garden while other coastal vegetation – sea grapes and railroad vine – helps protect the garden from the sea and prevent erosion.

The garden is bordered by another natural feature called the ghaut (pronounced gut) which is a natural, deep channel carrying vast quantities of rainwater down from Mount Nevis to the sea. One side of this deep channel has been reinforced with a wall of boulders, again to prevent erosion of the garden. Plants are kept watered during the dry season by an irrigation system although the pumps frequently burn out; the electricity company is short of funds and consequently the supply of power is erratic. Once plants establish in the tropics their rate of growth is rapid, which has meant that the garden has matured quickly, creating sheltered microclimates that enable other species to flourish. The mature planting now

The terrace around the pool is often used for relaxing, perhaps with a glass of wine or in the sheltered spa.

The warm buff textured coping stones and paving provide an excellent non-slip surface for wet feet around the swimming pool.

Shells litter the beach while a line of rocks indicates the position of an old jetty, destroyed by years of hurricanes.

outlines the lawn of soft zoysia grass and the pathways which wind down to the beach. Julie still visits once or twice a year to ensure that the planting is kept to a high standard, advising the gardeners on pest and disease control and pruning.

Seats are positioned around the garden to give views out across the sea to nearby islands, while two palm trees have been especially planted near the beach to support a hammock for lying and reading in the sun. Other palm trees planted around the garden will provide height and interest as well as much-needed shade.

Clive and Joy Bourne can now relax with friends surrounded by exotic plants and tropical birds in their island garden overlooking the sea. They host large barbecue parties in the garden and dinners on the veranda, which is decorated with gingers and heliconias cut from the garden – a hard-earned pleasure where nature was, and still remains, such a huge and unpredictable influence.

Ground rules

∗ Rapid plant growth means regular pruning, which is best

done before the hurricanes to minimise damage.

∗ Use trees and pergolas to provide plenty of shade

for both people and cars.

∗ Cut zoysia grass twice a week to prevent it forming hummocks.

∗ Apply fertiliser regularly as tropical soils are

quickly depleted of nutrients.

∗ Plant small palm trees which will quickly establish a strong

root system and so be more able to withstand hurricanes.

The shrub ixora with its red flowers and glossy foliage forms soft evergreen mounds under the palm trees next to the driveway.

Tropical fruits along with stunning plants, views and, of course, the climate combine to make this an idyllic island home.

There are frequent parties on the lawn as the warm weather means that more time is spent in the garden than indoors.

play

PLAY

The garden provides the ideal location for games and

RIGHT: Although a swimming pool is still a serious investment they have for many people become an integral part of outdoor family living. A rectangular in-ground pool, such as this, is ideal for serious swimming and the cool blue colour is certainly much more inviting to dive into than those black-lined pools with hidden depths.

Outdoor play certainly forms an important role in child development combining physical exercise, fun and learning within the stimulating environment of the garden. It is no longer the case that children are banished from the garden or escorted to the playground at the local park. In fact, many family gardens are now designed specifically with play in mind with special areas given over to children's play equipment, basketball nets and football goals, while even the smallest of gardens should at least have room to position a sandpit out of the way and perhaps a child's swing.

combines fresh air with fun for all the family.

The design of play areas within the garden will also be influenced by the age of the children. If you have very young children it is vital that they are kept under close supervision, and so a patio sited close to the house where they can ride tricycles or play with toys is an ideal solution. When children are older they will appreciate an area further away from the house where they can indulge in imaginative play without being overlooked. This could include a sandpit, as in my garden, partially hidden from the house by shrubs or trellis. Children can then progress to totally unsupervised play away from the house, possibly in secret gardens or in a small adventure playground completely hidden from view. The lawn, however, is one area where the whole family, from toddlers to grandparents, can come

together for games of French cricket or croquet, as well as being the main area for games at children's parties.

In addition to the lawn as the main family games area, very large gardens may also include more ambitious recreational features such as a tennis court or swimming pool. Large rural gardens may feature an orchard and areas of woodland in which children can play, while smaller spaces or urban gardens may be able to include a small copse of trees.

Water can also prove to be great fun and an additional area for learning through play if handled carefully. A shallow splash pool with a non-slip textured surface may be incorporated for fun, while children will always be enchanted by the secret world of a small garden pool.

Children will learn through play no matter what the location or how small the garden. The living world of plants and animals will encourage in children an active attitude of respect for their environment and other living creatures, and every garden will have a patch of ground where children can grow their own plants. Quick-growing, eye-catching plants are the most rewarding, as are those with flowers and berries that attract wildlife into the garden. Pets may also live outdoors, which in many ways is preferable to the house, for outside there is fresh air and probably more for the animal to look at from a hutch than when tucked in the corner of a room. Pets will form a rewarding part of family life, helping to teach children invaluable lessons about kindness and responsibility.

PLAY AREAS

When designing a garden for a young family, bear in mind that different games and activities will be suited to different areas of the garden. The lawn takes up the most space in the majority of gardens and this will probably form the main play area, as grass is the best surface for outdoor games. A small paved patio, however, might prove a more suitable area for young children, as they can sit outside in the sun and play with toys on a dry and level surface under the watchful eye of parents close by. Older children can also use this space for painting, drawing or reading.

PAVING AND PATIOS

Textured slabs or rough-surfaced bricks will give the best grip for little feet, but if you want paving that imitates natural stone try to choose one without too many variations in the surface as some are quite uneven and youngsters may find it hard to cope. It is essential that the patio is well laid without rocking or uneven paving as this could prove dangerous.

Patios are, of course, the perfect area for wheeled toys and tricycles. So, when you are planning your garden you may wish to consider extending an area of paving out from the main sitting area, or you may wish to lay a hard paved path all around the garden which will form a perfect cycle track. Low brick ramps built into the circuit will add to the fun and excitement of the

race around the track. At this planning stage, try to make sure that these paved areas are large enough for children to play on and will not constantly be covered in items of garden furniture, which can be most frustrating for young cyclists.

LAWNS

Lawns also need to be given some consideration. They should be laid from cultivated turf which will stand up to the wear-and-tear of family football games and other sporting activities. (Lawns can be grown from seed, which may be cheaper, but a playing surface will take far longer to establish and the results can often be quite disappointing.) Most gardens, even very compact spaces, will include a small area of grass, but make sure that this is not heavily shaded as you will find it

difficult to establish a lawn under these conditions and the area will become not much more than a patch of moss and mud.

Lawns are used for general play – running around, kicking a football, family games and children's party games – as well as quiet play like reading or playing cards on a blanket spread out under a tree. Level areas of lawn are best for most games, but where the lawn runs into a wilder area of longer grass then some mounding, either natural or man-made, will be great fun to roll down or as part of a bike track. Try not to scalp the grass too short when mowing your garden; longer grass actually looks better and is softer, but it is also less likely to scorch in dry weather and become bare and weed infested. Bowls and croquet are the only games that really need close-mown grass and, apparently, if croquet is played according to the proper rules then it not only needs finely cut grass but also a lawn the size of a tennis court. For many of us that may not be practical, not to mention being a bit too serious when really any area of lawn will suffice and a few humps and bumps will simply make the game more interesting. If you want to play either game seriously then you would be better off joining a club.

Play equipment is often sited together in one corner of the lawn; however, you may find that the grass wears out rapidly and can never really be satisfactorily repaired. Bark

Trees also provide the perfect props for rope bridges and swings, while allowing children to indulge in exciting and imaginative play well concealed from their parents' view. If your plot is relatively small you could always plant a few birch trees or other light foliage trees which will not make your garden too gloomy.

chippings provide a good alternative, particularly play-grade bark, which forms a suitably soft surface and is clean and free from splinters. All the play equipment can then be constructed together over a depth of bark chippings, which can simply be raked over and topped up when necessary. This type of surface looks particularly good in a shady setting where grass would probably not grow so well anyway. If you are lucky enough to have a small area of woodland in your garden, then that will form the perfect setting for just such an adventure playground. Woodland provides a totally different environment for adventurous play with bike tracks, games of hide-and-seek and the creation of dens and treehouses.

OPPOSITE: A hard paved path, preferably in textured paving, all round the garden will become an excellent cycle track into which you can always build low brick ramps to add to the excitement.

ABOVE LEFT: Most gardens will benefit from an area of lawn for running around, kicking a football or children's party games.

ABOVE RIGHT AND RIGHT: A wide range of well designed children's play equipment is now available including mini trampolines, swings and slides.

PLAY STRUCTURES

There are a few structures that are essential in a garden in order to tempt young children away from the television. The first of these is a sandpit, which can be the source of endless hours of uncomplicated enjoyment. It does not need to be big but it must be covered when not in use and should drain well to prevent the sand from turning into mud. A depth of approximately 30cm (12in) of silver sand is ideal. (Do not use builders' sand, as it will stain both skin and clothes.) An in-ground sandpit that finishes flush with surrounding paving will make better use of space than raised sandpits or those plastic varieties that fill up with water very quickly and have to be stored some-

where. When covered and not in use garden furniture can be used in this area or children can ride their tricycles over the top as an extension of their bike track.

Swings are another favourite and most people can find room for a swing somewhere in their garden. They may be constructed with a sturdy timber frame or can be made simply by securing a strong rope to an overhead branch and attaching a rubber tyre seat. Kit-form swings usually come in tubular steel and can be painted with special metallic paint to prevent rust. The factory fixing for this type of swing is only a driven metal spike, so you may find that as your children grow larger the swing begins to rock loose from the ground. In this case, it is possible to concrete each strut firmly into the ground to prevent the swing coming out of the ground completely, as it did in our garden – twice!

A rubber swing seat is safer than one made of timber or plastic, which may crack after a few years of use. Special baby swing seats – into which a toddler can be securely strapped – can also be bought, but you do still need to keep an eye on them. I once left one of our young boys rocking gently in one of these swings and when I next looked up I found, to my horror, that although he was still rocking back and forth he was also upside down.

Slides are good fun, too, but they do take up quite a lot of room and so may not be

Structured play areas

Ideally a sandpit should be built in at ground
level and covered with a lid to fit flush
with the surrounding paving. This means that
the area can be utilised for other
activities when the sandpit is not in use.

*

A swing can be constructed with a timber
frame to blend in with the surroundings.
It should always be positioned over an
area of grass or bark chippings for soft
landings. The use of bark chippings instead
of grass will prevent that unattractive area of
worn grass from appearing.

*

An area of textured paving, at least on two
sides of the garden, if not all the
way around, will provide children with a great
track on which to ride pedal cars
or bicycles.

OPPOSITE: Most gardens
will have room to construct
a swing either as a free-
standing frame or by
securing strong ropes to a
sturdy overhead branch.

LEFT: The curtains may be
drawn on this striped tent
to make a den or tied back
to leave a tunnel for the
children to run through.

ABOVE: This old hut in the
woods has been turned
into a delightful hideaway
for these two children
and their visiting chums
in the wheelbarrow.

Trampolines are great fun, too. They should be sited over a soft surface of grass or bark chippings and ideally there should be someone standing at each of the four sides to push any wayward gymnast back into the middle. Golf practice nets are also popular but they are not very aesthetic and are best suited to larger gardens where they can be masked by a backdrop of shrubs; they should also be situated away from neighbours' houses in case the net becomes frayed or works loose. Goal nets are similarly popular, although some of the tubular steel frames tend to fall apart and are a little unstable. Best of all is a wall where children can practise alone without having constantly to retrieve the ball. You may be fortunate enough to have a boundary wall that could be used but, if not, you could always build a free-standing wall from concrete blocks. If you paint a goal or a target on the wall it can be used for all sorts of sports including football, throwing skills, cricket or tennis.

The biggest feature in the garden, by far, is a tennis court which takes up a surprising

suitable for small gardens. A slide needs to be stable and have a soft surface all around, so the perfect solution is to set a slide on to a grass bank where it will sit firmly, with no drop at either side, and look less obtrusive than a free-standing slide. Climbing frames can also be cumbersome and expensive, and some of the more elaborate combinations on the market are a major investment. In many cases, it might be better to go to the park for this kind of activity, or if you feel up to it perhaps you could build your own adventure playground incorporating platforms, rope ladders, swings and slides. A blanket thrown over the equipment will offer welcome shade on a hot day while a tarpaulin can be used for shelter if it rains; both covers will, of course, create the perfect children's den.

It would go against the natural instincts of most children not to climb trees, so you will have to be vigilant when they start. The ideal tree will be strong and sturdy with a good open branch structure and a soft surface of grass or bark below it. Constructing a ladder up to a low-level platform in the tree, or even a treehouse, may encourage your children not to climb to dangerous heights. A simple platform can be turned into the perfect hiding place or den where they will enjoy spying on you from the seclusion of their leafy corner.

SPORTS EQUIPMENT

There is a huge range of sports equipment available for garden games including Swingball which is fun for tennis practice, and basketball nets, either free-standing or fixed to a wall. An outbuilding or garage wall is a better fixing point than a house wall, as the sound of the ball bouncing off it will reverberate through the house.

OPPOSITE TOP:
Trampolines are great fun
and are ideal for the
larger garden, where they
must be sited over
a soft surface of grass or
bark chippings.

OPPOSITE BELOW: A
blanket thrown over play
equipment or a pop-up
tent will form the perfect
children's den.

LEFT: A well-constructed
treehouse built in the
branches of a sturdy tree
forms the ultimate hide-
away and secret den for
children. A platform at this
level will perhaps deter
children from climbing any
higher up the tree.

amount of room. Although you do not need a space the size of Wimbledon's Centre Court you will still need an area of 33.5m x 16.46m (110ft x 54ft) which gives a 4.87m (16ft) run back at each end. Unless your court is on a perfectly flat site, you will also need to add an extra 1.5m (5ft) all around to allow for banks where the court is cut into a slope. If you do not have this extra room then you will need to construct retaining walls and this can be quite expensive. The ideal orientation for a tennis court – although it is not essential – is north–south, which keeps the awkward low morning and evening sun to the sides of the court.

Careful landscaping is required around a tennis court to ensure that it blends in with the surrounding garden. A high chain-link fence is especially difficult to mask although the height of the fence can be stepped down at the sides of the court to make it less obtrusive. Installing a tennis court can be a costly exercise, but it is a great investment for family life as tennis is one of those games that can be played by both young and old all year round.

WATER FEATURES

Water is another great source of amusement and pleasure in the garden and structures range from simple blow-up paddling pools to elaborate swimming pool complexes. Paddling pools can be folded away for storage and then brought out on to the lawn on hot sunny days, and some pools have an integral canopy to provide shade if the weather is just too hot. Shallow dish-shaped splash pools are great fun for children and can easily be installed into the ground. A surface of textured concrete provides a non-slip grip and a central drain (literally

a plug hole) empties the pool into a soak-away so there is no danger from a depth of standing water. Outdoor showers can be added to these pools for extra fun on hot days, along with jets of water shooting up from the pool itself.

Swimming pools are definitely back. However, now they are no longer the status symbol they once were, they have become an integral part of outdoor living for many families. Several factors have contributed to this change in attitudes: a higher standard of living, hotter summers and better technology which has resulted in stylish, affordable pool houses that allow all-year-round swimming. There has also been greater involvement on the part of garden designers when integrating the pool

into the garden, rather than relying on swimming pool companies who may have little interest in or knowledge of landscape design. Swimming pools are still, however, a serious investment when you consider the total cost of the construction of the pool, the pool house, pump house and paved terrace. You can go some way to reducing the cost by making use of the excavated soil for

ground shaping, which will save on paying for the soil to be taken away. An above-ground pool (literally sitting on the ground) is a cheaper installation than the more usual in-ground pool but there is nothing subtle about them and they are, in fact, very hard to blend into the landscape.

Rectangular pools – usually 9m x 4.5m (30ft x 15ft) in length – are useful for swimming lengths while free-form shapes are more suited to less serious swimming. Pools may be lined or tiled in whatever colour or pattern you want, but in general cool blue colours look more inviting than a pool with a dark or a black liner. These dark colours with wonderful reflective qualities may be fine for ornamental pools but not for a swimming pool. I prefer to dive into a clear pool where I can see the bottom rather than into a black lagoon with scary hidden depths.

It goes without saying that adults must be vigilant when youngsters are swimming but it will also help if textured, non-slip paving is laid around the pool and if low paling fencing, which is difficult to clumb, is constructed around the pool area to keep children out. Low-level lighting will illuminate the path to the pool and create an amazing atmosphere for evening poolside parties, while underwater lighting is essential for magical night-time swimming.

Swimming pool tips

A swimming pool is often a large and difficult shape to blend into the landscape so create a degree of harmony by linking the shapes of planting areas and terraces with the outline of your pool.

*

The height provided by shrub planting or raised beds around the pool terrace is essential to shelter swimmers from breezes.

*

The ideal site for an uncovered swimming pool is a sunny, open area with some shade around it.

*

Choose textured surfaces for swimming pool surrounds such as textured paving slabs, exposed aggregate concrete or resin-bonded aggregate. Rough-textured bricks also give grip while decking is warm underfoot and looks fantastic.

*

If your pool is at some distance from the house you will need to plan for additional changing facilities.

*

Walk-in pool steps are more attractive and easier for young children to manage than the bolt-on ladder type.

*

For reasons of safety it is usual for the shallow end of the pool to be nearest the entrance of the pool area.

GARDEN GAMES

Outdoor games may be completely unstructured, relying on the imagination and adventurous spirit of young children, or they may consist of all the rules and regulations of games like cricket and volley ball. Some games actually require a fair bit of organisation, in particular those played at children's birthday parties, where a constant supply of garden games is essential in order to avoid chaos.

From their early years, young children will play happily with a few toys scattered on a rug or even with a collection of empty cardboard boxes. Games do not have to be complicated to be fun and a prime example

of this is the sandpit. Sandpits nearly always prove to be a source of endless imaginative play as long as the sand is clean and dry and there are plenty of plastic shapes and buckets and some toy cars to push along tracks in the sand. A degree of supervision will inevitably be needed to ensure that the sand is not thrown around and over your children's little friends.

Other simple games include chasing round and round in circles, whether running or cycling around in pedal cars, so planned routes around the lawn, ideally on a paved track, will certainly be well used. Another favourite pastime of young children are games of hide-and-seek, which are possible even in the smallest of gardens as long as there are shrubs and garden buildings to hide behind. For young families such as these there is not really any point in growing

anything too precious, and you would always be well advised to keep sheds locked or at least to keep dangerous tools and chemicals out of reach.

ORGANISED GAMES

Bat-and-ball games such as rounders, football and cricket require few props to create the right structured environment for play. Similarly, basketball and netball require very little structure as all that is needed is a free-standing net or one that is fixed to a wall. A foldaway net can also be set up for informal games of tennis or badminton – which is excellent for family entertainment and fitness – although markers will be needed to give you some idea as to the length of the court.

If you have the space, there is no substitute for playing tennis on a proper court as an uneven lawn does not make for good rallies, which can be very frustrating for those just learning to play. However, a full-size tennis court does take up a lot of room and is expensive to install. Family games like cricket and volleyball will require some space on a lawn in order to be at a reasonable distance from neighbours' gardens to prevent the constant frustration of 'sixes' being hit over the fence.

OPPOSITE FAR LEFT: Not all play needs to be structured – a rug on the lawn with a few toys may be all that is needed.

OPPOSITE ABOVE AND BELOW: There are many garden games including hoopla and a variation of hopscotch played with numbered cards which can be bought today or even made yourself.

RIGHT: A foldaway net is great for family games of badminton or volleyball, with temporary markers to outline the court.

BELOW: Even something as simple as a garden sprinkler or hose can keep a toddler amused for hours as they run in and out of the spray or as they water the garden (or even their siblings!).

Two games where there should be no worry about balls disappearing over the fence are boules and croquet. Traditional boules is played in a special area of compacted gritty sand while croquet is played on an area of close-mown grass the size of a tennis court.

PARTY GAMES

Anyone who has ever hosted a children's birthday party will know how much planning is required and how many games need to be organised in order to keep the children occupied and amused. They will also know how quickly children go through a list of games, although somehow this does not seem to be quite such a problem outdoors where you can revert to ball games and hide-and-seek without the fear of damaged furniture and crockery. Contingency plans need to be made for the unpredictable summer weather, which may mean setting up a large tent in the garden or

ABOVE AND TOP RIGHT:
Grass is probably the best type of ground cover and the most suitable surface for play as it is soft, hard-wearing and extremely resilient. There is no doubt that a young family will give a lawn a fair amount of wear and tear, so it is important to lay a lawn that will be strong enough. Choosing turf containing dwarf rye grass is ideal as this is a particularly tough and slow-growing grass.

setting aside one room in the house to which everyone can retreat and shelter if there is a sudden downpour.

The partygoers can play in the sandpit or on the swing and climbing frame in addition to more structured games, many of which will be similar to those played indoors. A treasure hunt is good fun, with simple picture clues leading the children to different places in the garden and eventually to the treasure itself. One of the most successful treasure hunts I have seen was on a farm, where an adult read out each cryptic clue which sent the children scurrying off in different directions until one of them found the next hidden clue. This went on until the last clue was found and the winner was presented with the treasure.

LEFT AND OPPOSITE
BELOW: A level open area
of lawn is best for most
family games although
undulating areas, a wood-
land dell or an orchard can
all be fun for running
around, playing hide-and-
seek as well as other party
games. Croquet, however,
needs a fair-sized lawn
of close-mown grass to be
played seriously and
can probably only
be accommodated if there
are additional areas of
more hardwearing
lawn for other sports.

children an appetite before their lunch or birthday tea. After tea it might be a good idea for more traditional games, such as Pass the Parcel. We have played a variation on the game of Pin the Tail on the Donkey at a Pirate party by actually 'pinning' eyepatches on to a large picture of a pirate using Blutack. Other activities such as reading a story to the children can help to calm everyone down before they go home.

ABOVE LEFT AND RIGHT: If you are lucky enough to live by a lake or a river or if you have constructed a lake within your own garden, then this will create a whole new area of play. Model yachts and speedboats can be raced across the water and children could learn to row and canoe. Safety obviously has to be the top priority though and you will need to be vigilant at all times.

One of our favourite games is called Beach Flags, a game that we adapted from the original race we saw at a Surf Lifeguards' Championships at the beautiful Whitesands Bay in Pembrokeshire. The competitors were lined up at one end of a square court marked out on the sand, facing out in a press-up position, with everyone's feet on a line. On 'Go!' they would push up, spin round and race to the far end of the court to dive for one of the flags that had been set out in a line. Needless to say there was one less flag than competitors, so one person was eliminated after each race until there was only one winner left. This is really a variation on musical chairs, but it can be played on a lawn with either bean bags or tennis balls to pick up and from experience, the further you make the partygoers run the less frantic the game becomes. This sort of energetic game, as well as others like sack races, is useful in helping to give the

Garden games

Adventure play areas, especially in wooded areas, look good and can be great fun. Rope swings, treehouses and climbing frames can all be included and set over a wide base of bark chippings.

*

A wall built from blocks or bricks will allow children to practise football, tennis and other ball games on their own.

*

A basketball net can be used by one or more children and is best when either free-standing or fixed on to the garage wall to prevent noise from reverberating through the house.

*

A volleyball net on the lawn can be used for badminton and head tennis as well.

LEFT: Good planning is needed to ensure that a swimming pool is installed in harmony with its surroundings; here, shrubs and trees blend the pool into the garden and prevent unwelcome breezes from blowing across the water.

LEARNING THROUGH PLAY

Learning through outdoor play is a policy that has been taken on by many schools, whose once barren expanses of playground have now been converted into green spaces and small courtyards where children are encouraged to learn about plants and wildlife as well as to enjoy quiet reading time. This is a policy that could most certainly be adopted at home. In addition to the usual play areas of lawn and patio, an area may be set aside where children can learn to grow and care for plants such as nasturtiums, sweet peas and sunflowers, whose quick results will appeal to youngsters. Many of the ideas for this part of the garden will be similar to those for a sensory garden, where children will begin to appreciate eye-catching and fragrant flowers as

well as plants with interesting textures like the furry grey leaves of *Stachys byzantina* 'Silver Carpet'. Fragrant herbs are easy to grow as are certain fruit and vegetables including strawberries, carrots and radishes, and if the children can eat the produce as well as sowing the seeds and tending the plants then so much the better.

A sundial is another excellent addition to the garden. Placed in an open, sunny position it will help children to understand the concept of time and the movement of the sun. Children and adults, too, can begin to learn about different birds by planting trees and shrubs that will encourage them into the garden. The fruit of rowan and crab apple trees will attract birds while providing the additional seasonal interest of blossom

ABOVE: Young children will love to help with the jobs around the garden, which may then take a little longer but that does not matter as your children will be happy and out in the fresh air.

ABOVE: Encouraging children to work with you in the garden provides an opportunity for you to teach them about potential hazards and the safe handling of tools and equipment. Make the most of the young help and interest before they grow up.

LEFT: There are many berrying trees which attract birds into the garden and you can also help the process by making simple nesting boxes such as these in which they can seek refuge.

LEFT: Birds, bees and butterflies can all be encouraged into your garden by planting a variety of daisy flowers, such as sunflowers and asters, as well as buddleia, lilac, caryopteris and many other plants.

BELOW: Sowing seeds and growing fruit and vegetables will help children develop an interest in the environment but work such as this should definitely be fun and never a chore.

Encouraging learning in the garden

Plan in 'quiet' corners where children can sit and read or draw in a pleasant outdoor environment. Plants, birds and other wildlife as well as any views will give you plenty of good ideas for pictures.

*

A small patch of ground is all that is needed for children to grow their own radishes, carrots, nasturtiums and other plants. Plants that give quick and eye-catching results are the best for young children.

*

You do not need a special wildlife corner in order to encourage birds and butterflies – simply plant suitable shrubs throughout the garden such as buddleia and lavender or trees like rowan and crab apple.

*

There is a lot to be learnt from studying the magical world of a pond, which may be home to all sorts of animals like newts, tadpoles, frogs, waterboatmen and dragonflies.

and autumn colour. Many kinds of sunflower and aster will attract seed-eating birds, while others will be attracted by insects which can be found living on the silver birch tree. Netted tubes or hanging platform bird feeders can be positioned to provide food and encourage birds into the garden at times of the year when their natural supplies are scarce. You could help children to build a simple nesting box that will encourage birds to stay in the garden but the box must be positioned high up, out of the reach of predatory cats. Butterflies and bees will also be attracted to the garden if

OPPOSITE FAR LEFT:
Children will enjoy growing
plants such as sunflowers,
sweet peas and nasturtiums
along with other plants
which are quick to respond
and have eye-catching
results.

**OPPOSITE ABOVE AND
BELOW:** A sheltered corner
of the garden will be
an ideal place for young
children to grow a few
simple plants and possibly
to site a small animal run
for their pet.

LEFT: This fantastic
scarecrow would be great
fun for children
to make as well as serving
a useful purpose and
providing a humorous focal
point in the garden.

play

FAR LEFT AND LEFT: Birds will be encouraged into the garden by positioning netted tubes, hanging bird feeders and bird tables. In this way birds can be brought into the garden at times of the year when their natural supply of food is scarce.

you plant buddleia, caryopteris and lilac as well as the flowering current bush and many varieties of cotoneaster.

WATER AND WILDLIFE

Water is an attraction for both children and wildlife, so a shallow splash pool will offer the combined benefit of a paddling pool and bird bath as well. When children are beyond the toddling stage a small pond can be incorporated in the garden, complete with newts, tadpoles and dragonflies. The large leaves of water lilies will provide shade for fish and children can learn about the different types of plant that grow in water and about those that grow in a moist bog garden, too. Although there is some work involved in maintaining a pond to keep it free from algae and blanket weed and to establish oxygenating plants to create the right balance in the water, there is no doubt that a small water garden can be a fascinating world of its own.

Encouraging learning in the garden is fun and rewarding for both you and your children; a notepad and a collecting jar is all you need. Small areas for flowers and vegetables, marked out with pebbles collected from the beach, will add to the fun while growing plants that can be eaten will give pleasure and a clearer understanding that food does not just come in a plastic wrapping from supermarket shelves. Children will also see that plants attract wildlife into the garden and this will begin to put them in touch with the natural world – a place that many of them never learn about and are in danger of forgetting when their life revolves around a computer and a television screen.

RIGHT AND BOTTOM RIGHT: Great fun can be had with the simplest of equipment – a jam jar is all that is needed for pond dipping and children can discover the secret world that lies under the water's surface inhabited by tadpoles, beetles and snails.

OPPOSITE BELOW: This galvanised metal trough has been converted into a raised pool full of aquatic plants which provide cover for a fascinating miniature world of wildlife.

LEFT: A large pond bordered by reeds and dense planting may be home to wildfowl, shrews and voles as well as frogs and toads.

TOP RIGHT: Sitting on a deck by the water's edge, pushing an apple through the water with sticks, the simplest of activities, has held these three young children captivated.

PETS

ABOVE AND RIGHT: Pets can be great companions, extremely rewarding and can help children learn respect for other living creatures. It is, however, an enormous responsibility to own and care for a pet so you would be wise to do plenty of research before taking one on.

In addition to wildlife, your garden may be home to domestic animals like the family dog or a couple of rabbits. There is no doubt that great pleasure can be derived from owning pets and that children will also learn some valuable lessons, including the responsibility of animal husbandry and a respect for other living creatures.

Rabbits are very popular as pets and have an advantage in that they can quite easily be housed outdoors. This keeps the mess outside and is better for your furniture, but just because the animal is out of sight it should obviously not be forgotten. Apart from the regular care that is needed, rabbits like attention and they will actually begin to suffer if they are neglected for too long. An outdoor hutch needs to be sited so that it protects the rabbit from cold winds, high temperatures and rainfall. A position close to a house wall will shield the hutch from icy winds, while the overhang of a porch may offer welcome shade and shelter from driving rain. If your garden is completely bordered by solid fencing and you are sure that it is rabbit proof, then you can allow your rabbit to run around on the lawn for exercise. This is probably not a good idea if you have a large garden with plenty of hiding places as it may take a long time to retrieve your pet. It may be a better idea to put the rabbit into a portable run, which can then be moved around the lawn so that one area does not get completely

worn out. Rabbits are, of course, great burrowers so a sheet of netting at the base of the run will allow grass to poke through and be nibbled while, at the same time, preventing the lawn from being scratched up and the rabbit from breaking free.

Dogs can also be kept outside in a kennel with a run as long as the construction allows the dog to move around easily and the site has some shade and is protected from draughts. Dogs do need regular exercise. For puppies this may simply be a run around the garden, but more mature animals will need to be walked a good distance each day. Letting puppies play in the garden requires the same vigilance that you would give to young children. The area needs to be completely safe, which means that gates must be kept shut and all

boundaries must be secure. Ponds are not a good idea but if you do have one then fence it off until the dog is older. Puppies will be unaware of potential dangers and may well seek out cool shade under your car, so if you do let your puppy out be sure you know where it is before moving the car. Bottles of chemicals and sharp objects must also be locked away or kept high up in a shed out of harms way.

PRACTICALITIES

If you are considering owning other animals such as chickens, rare breed pigs, goats and other livestock, it all gets a lot more serious. You may find that local by-laws restrict you from keeping certain animals in your garden so that would have to be investigated before you start building pens and hen houses. There will also be a lot of health issues to check both for the sake of the animals you intend to keep and for other people if you intend passing on produce like eggs and milk to the public.

Keeping pets in the garden is a way of life for some families who find it extremely rewarding. It is, however, a huge responsibility to care for animals and although it may seem quite idealistic to keep a couple of rabbits and have chickens scratching around in the back yard, it can also be expensive and is incredibly demanding on your time. Pets need care and attention every day of the year, no matter what the weather, so you will need to do your research and be fully informed about what you are taking on before including animals as part of your outdoor living.

TOP AND ABOVE: Gerbils, hamsters and rabbits are popular pets and reasonably easy to look after while chickens, goats and other livestock may be subject to quite a few health issues; in addition, you will need to check out any local restrictions which concern the owning of certain animals.

BIRD TABLE

A bird table like this one is a really simple construction and yet it brings such pleasure to see birds coming into the garden to feed during the winter time. If birds are actually going to use your table, though, it must be well positioned in a fairly open spot away from overhanging branches and fences where predatory cats may prowl. For this same reason, it should be high enough off the ground, with a supporting pole of smooth wood that is difficult for both cats and squirrels to climb. Although specific sizes have been indicated in our project, you really can use any off-cuts of timber as long as they are clean and free from sharp edges. The bird table should also be sturdy and well treated with a water-based preservative. Avoid the rustic designs that are sold in garden centres as not only will they not last but also the rough pole is easy for cats to climb. The table should be kept clean of old food and periodically treated with a preservative. For added interest, you could always carve your own wooden bird to fix on to the side.

MATERIALS

* Length of sawn timber 7.5cm x 2.5cm (3in x 1in) for the sides and base support. For this, a length approximately 1.8m (6ft) long will leave a piece of about 20cm (8in) from which to shape your wooden bird
* 1.25cm (½in) thick exterior grade plywood to be cut to a rectangle 30cm x 27.5cm (12in x11in)
* Sturdy wooden pole, approximately 3.8cm (1½in) in diameter or a wooden post 3.8cm x 3.8cm (1½ x1½in). Overall length to be 1.8–2.1m (6–7ft)
* Wood glue
* About 15 galvanised nails, 5cm (2in) long
* Water-based exterior wood preservative

TOOLS

* Panel saw
* Sandpaper
* Pencil
* Power drill and wood bits
* Club hammer
* Workbench
* Wood chisels
* Wood mallet
* Old paint brush
* Jig saw

1 Cut the length of timber into sections 32.5cm (13in) long to form the sides. Hold them firm on a workbench while you nail them together using galvanised nails; you may find it easier to fix three sides and to glue the plywood base into place before fixing on the fourth. Leave a gap of 2.5cm (1in) in the base of the table for drainage.

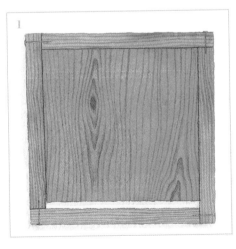

2 Cut a further length of timber 32.5cm (13in) to form the base support for the table. Mark the centre of this timber and pencil a circle around this point which is the same diameter as the wooden pole. Hold the timber firm on a workbench and cut out the circle of wood you have just marked. You can do this by drilling a series of connecting holes in the wood and then completing the job with wood chisels and sandpaper to form one smooth hole.

3 Glue around the end of the pole and knock the base support on to it prior to fixing it to the table. If the pole is going to be driven into the ground, then do not glue on the base support but simply ensure that it fits.

4 Turn the table upside down and nail on the base support and pole using galvanised nails. If the pole has already been driven into the ground, then once the base support has been nailed to the table simply glue it on to the top of the pole. A couple of nails through the plywood table into the top of the pole will hold it firm. If the bird table and pole are to be installed as one unit, then first spike a hole into the lawn and push the pole into it; you may find that a bucketful of concrete will help to hold it firm. As a finishing touch a wooden bird could be glued to the table prior to treating the whole structure with preservative.

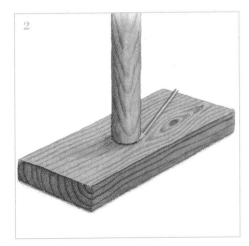

SANDPIT

A sandpit is a must for families with young children and can provide hours of entertainment in the summer. It really does not need to be enormous either, for the one shown here, only about 90cm (3ft) by 120cm (4ft), is actually in our garden and I once counted eight children, all playing happily in it together. This type of sandpit that is set into the ground also makes good use of space as when it is not in use it can be covered over completely, allowing you to walk on it and use the area as an extension of the patio. The timber lids are essential to keep cats out of the sand and should always be put back on it when play has finished. Rainwater will filter through the gaps in the lids and into the sand, where it will drain into the hardcore underneath which acts as a soakaway. If, however, your garden is permanently waterlogged you may find it more satisfactory to build a raised sandpit.

MATERIALS

* About 0.25cu m (2.76cu ft) free-draining clean hardcore or large aggregate shingle
* Sheet of geotextile drainage membrane or fine mesh netting approximately 1.8m x 2.1m (6ft x 7ft) in size
* About 0.5 cu m (5.52cu ft) concrete
* 200 well-fired, frostproof bricks including four specially shaped cant bricks
* 10 brick wall butterfly ties
* 1 barrowful of mortar
* 5m (16ft) length of 5cm x 5cm (2in x 2in) prepared timber
* 7.3m (24ft) total length of 15cm x 2.5cm (6in x 1in) prepared timber
* 50 galvanised nails, 5cm (2in) long
* Tin of suitable colour wood stain
* 8–10 bags of playsand

TOOLS

* Spade
* Shovel
* Wheelbarrow
* 3m (10ft) steel tape
* Brick trowel
* String line
* Spirit level
* Short length of copper pipe or hosepipe for smoothing brick joints
* Panel saw
* Claw hammer

ABOVE: Try to make your in-ground sandpit finish flush with the surrounding paving, as you can use the area as an extension of the patio.

RIGHT: A well-constructed sandpit will provide endless hours of enjoyment for young children; be sure to use silver sand as builder's sand will stain both skin and clothes.

1 Dig out an area 1.575m x 1.35m (5ft 3in x 4ft 6in) to a depth of about 32.5cm (13in) and remove the soil. After marking the positions for the side walls, dig out an extra 15cm (6in) for the concrete footings. Build up the four brick courses to form the sandbox, setting in the wall ties at even spacing round the first two courses. The inside and top face of the top two brick courses may be seen, so finish the joints by rubbing them smooth with a bucket handle or short section of pipe. After the brickwork has set firm, you can dig out a further 20–25cm (8–10in) lower than the base of the footings, over the area of the sandpit. Remove the soil and backfill this area with clean hardcore or large aggregate shingle. Cover this stone with a fine mesh net or geotextile membrane to allow drainage without losing the sand; the net also prevents the stones from getting in.

2 Take the concrete and pour it behind the walls to bind firm with the wall ties. This will provide strength without the cost or time involved from building an extra skin of brickwork. Lay a brick on edge trim on mortar, over this concrete around the outside of the brick box. The brick trim will finish flush with surrounding paving on the outside. Set four specially shaped bricks called cant bricks

into the brick trim at one end of the sandpit to provide a finger hole for removing the timber lid.

3 Make up the lid in two halves as one complete lid is too heavy. Make up a framework of 5cm x 5cm (2in x 2in) prepared timber for each lid with the width of the timber frame the same as the width between the side walls of the sandpit. Then cut timber boards which are 15cm x 2.5cm (6in x 1in) to the width between the side brick trims and nail them firmly on to the timber frame. A gap of about 0.6cm (¼in) between each board will allow for expansion of the timber when wet. Treat all the timber with an exterior wood stain.

4 Lay the drainage membrane, over the hardcore, and fold it up against the sides of the sandpit. After making sure all the brickwork has been cleaned up you can now pour in the sand up to the top course of bricks. It is important to allow an air gap under the timber so it can breathe and does not sit on damp sand. You will probably need to top up the sandpit every year, especially if it has been well used throughout the summer. (And however much care you take with little sandy feet you will be amazed at how much sand gets into the house!)

BOULES—SKITTLES

This is a simple game that combines boules and skittles and can be played with a variety of rules on a surface of dry sand, grass or paving. The balls can be used on their own to play boules or they could be used to knock down the tin cans in a variation of the game of skittles.

In this latter case, each player could have two balls of the same colour to knock down as many cans as possible, setting up the cans again for each player. The winner could be the player who knocks over the greatest number of cans or the one who has scored the highest number of points as marked on the side of the cans. This is an ideal game for three or four players but if there are only two playing they could, perhaps, have four balls each.

Making the game is a great activity for a rainy day and children will probably enjoy the making of the game just as much as they will enjoy playing with it later.

ABOVE: Children will enjoy this game which combines elements of boules with skittles, especially if they have made it themselves.

RIGHT: Garden games can be made out of almost anything and here beach pebbles have been painted with letters to make a crossword.

MATERIALS

* ★ 10 clean tin cans
* ★ Stiff card or paper
* ★ Gloss paint or paint for metal surfaces
* ★ Coloured tissue paper
* ★ Large box of thick elastic bands, all the same size

TOOLS

* ★ Metal file
* ★ Paint brushes
* ★ Oil-based marker pen
* ★ Scissors
* ★ Pencil
* ★ Masking tape

LEFT: There is a huge number of garden games you can play ranging from organised sports such as cricket, badminton and volleyball through to less structured activities like this game of skittles, which requires only a small space on a level area of lawn and may be played by one person alone.

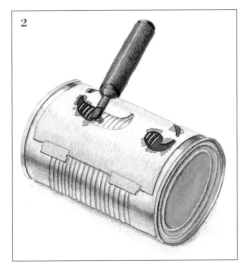

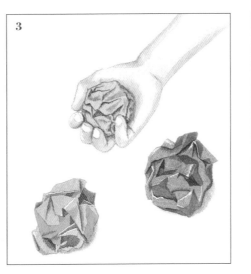

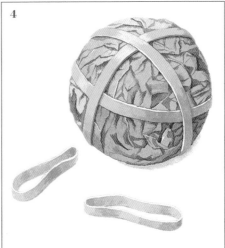

1 Carefully ensure that there are no sharp edges on the tin cans you have saved, using a metal file where necessary around the rim of the can. Make sure that the cans are completely clean and dry before painting the insides with brightly coloured gloss or metal paint, if desired. If your children are doing the painting, check that there isn't paint swimming around at the bottom of the cans before putting them out of reach to dry overnight.

2 Make your own number stencils from stiff card or paper. Use masking tape to stick the stencils on to each can and then carefully draw on the numbers using a brightly coloured oil-based marker pen.

3 Use layers of coloured tissue paper, rolled and squeezed tightly, to form the balls. Build up the layers of paper until you have a round firm ball about the size of those that are used in a game of boules. Make two balls of the same colour for each person. The balls may be made more durable by wrapping each of them in a trimmed section of a clear plastic bag before adding the elastic bands.

4 Stretch the elastic bands around the tissue ball, adding more and more bands until you have a firm rigid sphere but can still see the coloured tissue paper. Keep the game in the dry when not in use so that it lasts for longer.

the bohm-duchens, **a town garden**

Michael and Monica Bohm-Duchen moved into their home in Hampstead, London, about ten years ago shortly before their daughter, Hannah, was born. Theirs is a tall, Victorian terraced house on four floors with a roof terrace and a conservatory. The garden, which is seventy feet long, is typical of the area – long and narrow, shaded by neighbouring houses and tall poplar trees, with an acid soil in which camellias, rhododendrons and azaleas all thrive. The size and character of the garden were certainly influential factors in the choice of this property, as was the close proximity to the wide open spaces of Hampstead Heath which are wonderful for long walks and large-scale ball games that are too much for the garden.

Michael is a professor at London University where he teaches physiology. He is a keen horticulturist and enjoys spending time in the garden. His other great passion is for cooking and he combines the two by preparing many barbecue meals for family and friends on the patio.

ABOVE: Lunchtime snacks and party teas are commonplace in the Bohm-Duchen garden as the children's friends will often come around to play.

LEFT: The patio, which has been laid simply to gravel, leads out on to the lawn under a timber pergola covered with climbing roses, clematis and wisteria.

RIGHT: The play frame, which is concealed among dense planting at the far end of the garden, was purpose-built by hand to be exactly as the children wanted.

Monica is a freelance art historian, writer and organiser of exhibitions. She likes to give occasional help outside but above all she loves to watch her two children playing in the garden. The oldest child, Hannah, is ten and is keen on reading, acting and music while her brother, Benji, who is seven and boisterous, enjoys ball games and probably tests the durability of the garden to its limits.

When the Bohm-Duchens first took on their new garden, they found that both the layout and the choice of plants were rather formal and that the sitting-out area was far too small for their needs. Michael proceeded to soften the formality with new planting but after a couple of years he found that the space was becoming too overgrown and crowded and that, in fact, many of the new plants he had tried were struggling. So Michael and Monica reworked their ideas and, with professional assistance, they set about redesigning and building their new garden.

Access into the garden from the back door has always been difficult as it involved climbing a flight of steps which was both narrow and steep. These were rebuilt to be broader and shallower and altogether much safer. The Bohm-Duchens are still considering a greater improvement to the access, out of the kitchen at the back of the house, although this would involve some major construction work. The patio area was enlarged and laid simply to gravel with some random stone slabs, all softened with planting and enhanced by a wonderful Japanese maple. A water feature was built close to the patio where water bubbles through sea urchins, sculpted by Dennis Fairweather, before it falls into a shingle surround and then into two lower, brick-built pools. A play area was introduced for the children further down the garden. Michael also removed the tired roses which he had planted two years previously and replaced them with much more suitable ferns and hellebores.

In addition to the main steps, there is also rope access on to the play frame which brings you up through a trap door.

Water falls into two brick-built pools to create a soothing feature and focal point next to the secluded and intimate patio.

The play frame has been ideal for the energetic Benji, who constantly charges up and down the steps and across the timber bridge.

Access into the rest of the garden is under a timber pergola heavy with roses, clematis and wisteria. The garden opens on to a lawn, softened by shrubs, leading on to the children's play frame. There are steps up to the frame and a rope which the children climb to emerge through a trap door. There is also a scramble net which is attached to the frame and the whole construction has been built by hand so that it is just as they wanted it. A shed was hidden away at the end of the garden to store the children's toys.

The Bohm-Duchens have developed a wonderful family garden in which they can entertain all their friends. Despite the city location, Michael has learnt to treat the garden as a woodland environment because of the shady conditions. He still battles to establish new plants but he has learnt to compromise and to accept that sacrifices in horticultural excellence must be made in a family garden where young children run, climb and kick footballs every day.

Ground rules

* *Plan sufficient storage space to avoid clutter.*

* *Create areas where children may play in safety away from less robust planting.*

* *Patio areas should be large enough for family and friends to sit and enjoy a meal in comfort.*

* *The patio should be easily accessible from the house and provide easy access to the rest of the garden.*

* *Choose plants to suit the soil and aspect of the garden.*

Water emerges through the sea urchins sculpted by Dennis Fairweather, then falls into the two lower pools of this well-designed water feature.

On summer days Hannah and Benji will often share a snack up in their secret hideout which is camouflaged by shrubs.

A wonderful family garden has been created by the Bohm-Duchens who have learnt the art of balancing horticulture with children's play.

the hepworths, **wonderland garden**

Elton Hall, situated near Ludlow in Herefordshire, was originally built in the seventeenth century and has been the home of James and Anne Hepworth for the past seventeen years. They live there with their two children, who are affectionately called Puffin and Pelican, and a menagerie of animals including several cats and dogs, guinea pigs, hamsters, chickens, horses and Highland cattle. The children also keep pet tortoises in a fantastic brick-built fortress while Hebridean sheep reside in a Moorish-style palace.

The garden has developed as a fascinating and intriguing mix of quirky architecture and extremely bold, well structured areas of planting. It is an adventureland garden which has become the most amazing place for the two girls to grow up in, play with their pets, and indulge in childhood fantasies and games of make believe.

ABOVE: There are many curious figures positioned around the grounds of Elton Hall; here a tall carved soldier towers above Pelican, who makes a salute.

LEFT: The garden is a huge playground for the Hepworths' two daughters who take time out from play to relax in this ornate garden building.

RIGHT: The miniature palace at the end of the mown path is just one of the numerous follies to have been built and which make this garden such an incredible fantasy land.

There is a castle and miniature palace, ornamental play houses, meadows to run through and a vast array of animals to care for. The development of the garden has been the work of a unique partnership between the Hepworths, their head gardener, Anthony Brooks, and Ted Wade who built the incredible follies. James Hepworth is an art and property dealer who has collected and installed the strangest items within the garden in the most creative way. James breaks all the rules of garden design, ignoring the need for a master plan but instead acting on impulse and following whims and fancies; Gothic moods have led to Gothic structures while a desire for Moorish architecture resulted in the Moorish sheep palace.

When Anthony Brooks joined the Hepworths nine years ago he began to build the garden around the unusual structures which were in existence at that time. Anthony is no follower of convention either, avoiding traditional herbaceous borders in favour of planting schemes which echo a natural habitat. He uses tall grasses like *Stipa gigantea* to create movement in beds of summer flowering rudbeckias and kniphofias. He has brought a greater structure and sense of order to the garden with his inspired planting design, the opening-up of vistas and linking of areas with pathways.

The gardens are about 2.5 hectares (6 acres) in total and contain among other things a national collection of echinaceas and rudbeckias. There is also a large kitchen garden with a fully restored Victorian glasshouse and a herb garden, the entrance to which is guarded by two cast-iron elephants. The gardens are also home to some very old fruit trees which were planted by an illustrious former owner of Elton Hall. Thomas Andrew Knight was a founder member and President of the Horticultural Society which later became the Royal Horticultural Society. Knight moved to Elton Hall in 1791 where he dedicated much of his time to breeding fruit, having

The cat in the arms of the Hepworths' eldest daughter, Puffin, is just one of the many animals to be found at Elton Hall.

This small playhouse has been built for the children and made even more homely by the low rustic fence and the pots of flowering plants.

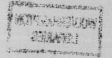

particular success with cherries including 'Elton Heart' and 'Waterloo' which apparently first fruited just before the battle.

The Hepworths make good use of the space within the garden to host summer parties while for the children it is just like a fantasy land. The garden is full of surprises straight out of a fairy story: a tall carved soldier stands to attention at the base of a tree while tin soldiers can be found in other hideouts. There is even a carved stone puffin in honour of one of the girls. A delivery of two chandeliers ordered from Australia arrived in large wooden crates; the crates have since been positioned near the back of the house with tin roofs attached to become playhouses.

The gardens, which are a fantastic mixture of follies, exquisite planting and a children's playground, do not stay still for long; a water feature is planned, to be followed by a grotto, and who knows what other strange and wondrous buildings may appear.

Ground rules

Avoid using a master plan, leaving you free to develop ideas and features at will.

Build and improve on the existing framework within the garden.

Ensure that the garden accommodates every member of the family.

Be creative – the most unusual things can be adapted for use in the garden.

Ignore the rules.

A splendid brick fortress with castellations, sturdy gates and cannon positions is also the fortified home of the children's pet tortoises.

The fortress is better than most play equipment with the walls making the perfect climbing frame and enabling Pelican to practise her balancing skills.

187

suppliers and addresses

GARDEN DESIGNERS

Richard Key Landscape Design
40 Glenham Road
Thame
Oxfordshire OX9 3WD
Tel/Fax. 01844 213051
Email: richard@richardkey.co.uk
www.richardkey.co.uk

Society of Garden Designers
Katepwa House
Ashfield Park Avenue
Roos on Wye
Herefordshire HR9 5AX
Tel. 01989 566695

LANDSCAPE CONTRACTORS

Adam Frost
Duncombs Farm, Little Bytham
Grantham, Lincolnshire NG33 4QN
Tel. 01780 410926

South Hills Landscape
Pond House, Hogshaw
Buckingham
Buckinghamshire MK18 3LB
Tel. 01296 670520

Farrscape
43 Harries Way, Holmer Green
High Wycombe
Buckinghamshire HP15 6UE
Tel. 01494 712619

BRICKS

**Freshfield Lane
Brickworks Ltd**
Dane Hill
Haywards Heath
Sussex RH17 7HH
Tel. 01825 790350

**The York Handmade Brick
Company**
Forest Lane, Alne
North Yorkshire YO6 2LU
Tel. 01347 838881

CONCRETE PAVING

Atlas Stone Products Ltd
Westington Quarry
Chipping, Campden
Gloucestershire GL55 6EG
Tel. 01386 841104

Camas Building Materials
Hulland Ward
Ashbourne
Derbyshire DE6 3ET
Tel. 01335 372244

Marshalls Mono Ltd
Southowram
Halifax HX3 9SY
Tel. 01422 306355

Stonemarket
Old Gravel Quarry
Oxford Road
Ryton on Dunsmore
Warwickshire CV8 3EJ
Tel. 024 7630 5530

Town and Country Paving
Unit 10 Shrublands Nurseries
Roundstone Lane
Angmering, Littlehampton
West Sussex BN16 4AT
Tel. 01903 776297

NATURAL STONE

Civil Engineering Developments Ltd
728 London Road
West Thurrock, Grays
Essex RM20 3LU
Tel. 01708 867237

Silverland Stone
Holloway Hill
Chertsey
Surrey KT16 0AE
Tel. 01932 569277

SELF SETTING GRAVEL

Breedon plc
Breedon on the Hill
Derby DE73 1AP
Tel. 01332 862254

RESIN BONDED SURFACE DRESSING

**Addagrip Surface
Treatments UK Ltd**
Bird-in-Eye Hill
Uckfield
East Sussex TN22 5HA
Tel. 01825 761333

DECKING

Leisuredeck Limited
311 Marsh Road
Leagrave, Luton
Bedfordshire LU3 2RZ
Tel. 01582 563080

FENCING

Blenheim Palace Sawmill
Combe
Witney
Oxfordshire OX8 8ET
Tel. 01993 881206

Forest Fencing
Standford Court
Standford Bridge
Worcestershire WR6 6SR
Tel. 01886 812451

HillHout Ltd
Unit 3 Salmon Road
Great Yarmouth
Norfolk NR30 3QS
Tel. 01493 332226

**HS Jackson and Son
(Fencing) Ltd**
75 Stowting Common
Ashford
Kent TN25 6BN
Tel. 01233 750393

**M & M Timber
Company Ltd**
Hunt House
Sawmills, Clows Top
Kidderminster
Worcestershire DY14 9HY
Tel. 01299 832 611

GARDEN STRUCTURES

Agriframes Ltd
Charlwoods Road
East Grinstead
West Sussex RH19 2HP
Tel. 01342 310000

Alitex
Station Road, Alton
Hampshire GU34 2PZ
Tel. 01420 82860

Amdega Ltd
Faverdale, Darlington
County Durham DL3 0PW
Tel. 01325 468522

The Garden Trellis Company
Unit 1, Brunel Road
Gorse Lane Industrial Estate
Clacton on Sea, Essex CO15 4LU
Tel. 01255 688361

Stuart Garden Architecture
Burrow Hill Farm
Wiveliscombe
Somerset TA4 2RN
Tel. 01984 667458

DECORATIVE WOOD PROTECTION

Salodin UK Ltd
Salodin House
Meadow Lane, St Ives
Cambridgeshire PE17 4UY
Tel. 01480 496868

RECLAIMED MATERIALS

Dorset Reclamation
Cow Drove
Bere Regis, Wareham
Dorset BH20 7JZ
Tel. 01929 472200

SWIMMING POOLS

**Swimming Pool and Allied
Trades Association Ltd**
SPATA House
Junction Road, Andover
Hampshire SP10 3QT
Tel. 01264 356210

LIGHTING

Lighting Alfresco
The Cottage, Slade End
Brightwell cum Sotwell
Oxfordshire OX10 0RQ
Tel. 01491 826025

PLANTS

Acorn (MK) Nurseries
Newton Road
Emberton, Olney
Buckinghamshire MK46 5JW
Tel. 01234 713469

Waddesdon Gardens Ltd
Queen Street
Waddesdon
Buckinghamshire HP18 0JW
Tel. 01296 651287

Waterperry Gardens Ltd
Waterperry
Nr Wheatley, Oxford OX33 1JZ
Tel. 01844 339254

BULBS

OA Taylor and Sons Bulbs Ltd
Washway House Farm
Holbeach, Spalding
Lincolnshire PE12 7PP
Tel. 01406 422266

TURF

Rolawn Ltd
Elvington
York YO4 5AR
Tel. 01842 828266

GRASS SEED

Johnsons Seeds
London Road
Boston
Lincolnshire PE21 8AD
Tel. 01205 365051

FURNITURE

Barlow Tyrie Ltd
Braintree
Essex CM7 2RN
Tel. 01376 322505

Indian Ocean Trading Company
155-163 Balham Hill
London SW12 9DJ
Tel. 020 8675 4808

PLANTERS

Christian Day Ltd
Unit 2, Building 329
Rushock
Droitwich Road, Droitwich
Worcestershire WR9 0NR
Tel. 01299 250385

Cranborne Stone
West Orchard, Shaftesbury
Dorset SP7 0LJ
Tel. 01258 472685

Pots and Pithoi
The Barns
East Street
Turners Hill
West Sussex RH10 4QQ
Tel. 01342 714793

Whichford Pottery
Whichford, Shipston-on-Stour
Warwickshire CV36 5PG
Tel. 01608 684416

SCULPTURE

Croft Studios
Unit 6 High Street, Stourbridge
West Midlands DY8 1DE
Tel. 01384 393389

Fairweather Sculpture
Hillside House, Starston
Norfolk IP20 9NN
Tel. 01379 852266

Simon Percival
Sunnymead Works
Toadsmoor Road
Brimscombe
Gloucestershire GL5 2UF
Tel. 01453 731478

Mark Richard Hall
Crumble Cottage
Crossroads
Woodlands
Wimborne
Dorset BH21 8LP
Tel. 01202 813631

GARDEN ACCESSORIES

The Conran Shop
Michelin House
81 Fulham Road
London SW3 6RD
Tel. 020 7589 7401

Habitat
Tel. 0845 60 10 740
for nearest store

McCord
Tel. 0870 90 87 020
for mail order

**Ocean Home
Shopping Ltd**
Tel. 0870 24 26 283
for mail order

acknowledgments

Conran Octopus would like to thank the following photographers and organisations for their kind permission to reproduce the photographs in this book:

1 Andreas von Einsiedel/Country Homes & Interiors/IPC Syndication; **2-3** William Abranowicz/Art & Commerce Anthology Inc; **5** Esto/Mark Darley (Mary Griffin); **6 left** Tim Beddow/Conran Octopus (Kathryn Ireland); **6 right** Debbi Treloar/Homes & Gardens/IPC Magazines; **6 centre** Mark Darley/Esto; **7 left** Richard Imrie/Conran Octopus; **7 right** Tim Beddow/Conran Octopus (Kathryn Ireland); **7 centre** S & O Mathews; **8** Fritz von der Schulenburg/The Interior Archive (Mimmi O'Connell); **9** Marianne Majerus/Conran Octopus (Elton Hall); **10 above** Juliette Wade/Conran Octopus (Cheryl Cummings); **10 below** Harpur Garden Library (D Warmflash); **11** James Merrell/Homes & Gardens/IPC Magazines; **12** Harpur Garden Library (Oehme & van Sweden); **13** Harpur Garden Library (Simon Hopkinson); **14 above** Harpur Garden Library/Marcus Harpur (Jonathan Baillie); **14 below** John Glover (Steven Woodhams); **15** Harpur Garden Library; **16 above** Andrew Wood/ The Interior Archive (Philip Hooper); **16 below** Gary Rogers/Tummers; **17** Marianne Majerus/The Garden Picture Library (Haseley Court); **18 above** Harpur Garden Library (Chris Rosmini, Los Angeles); **18 below** Harpur Garden Library (Tom Carruth & John Furman); **19 above** Deidi von Schaewen; **19 below left** Gary Rogers (Henk Weijers); **19 below right** Harpur Garden Library (Martina Barzi & Josefina Casares); **20 above** Gary Rogers/Jona Pietzka; **20 below** Gary Rogers/Crabtree & Evelyn, Chelsea Flower Show (Jane Fearnley-Whittingstall); **21 left** Deidi von Schaewen; **21 right** Harpur Garden Library (Keeyla Meadows); **22** Howard Rice/The Garden Picture Library (Kiftsgate Court); **23** Marianne Majerus (The Japanese Garden, Notts); **23 right** Deidi von Schaewen; **24** Andrew Lawson (Old Rectory Sudborough); **25 above left** Harpur Garden Library (Sonny Garcia, San Francisco); **25 below left** Juliette Wade/The Garden Picture Library; **25 below right** Deidi von Schaewen; **26-27** Simon Kenny/Vogue Living; **27 above** Clive Nichols/Nichols Garden, Reading; **27 below right** Clive Nichols (Fisher Price Garden/Sarah Eberle Hampton Court 1998); **28 above left** Jacqui Hurst/The Garden Picture Library; **28 above right** Jerry Pavia/The Garden Picture Library; **28 below** Ron Sutherland/The Garden Picture Library (B Sweerts); **29 left** Andrew Lawson; **29 right** Brigitte Thomas/The Garden Picture Library; **30** Brigitte Thomas/The Garden Picture Library; **31 above** Gary Rogers/Christopher Carter, Filkins; **31 below** Claire Davies/The Garden Picture Library; **32-33 above** Juliette Wade (Thorpe Hall, Roffe); **32-33 below** Mark Bolton/The Garden Picture Library (Willow Lodge); **33** Juliette Wade (York Gate); **34 left** Clive Nichols (Sticky Wicket, Dorset); **34 below** Marcus Harpur/Harpur Garden Library (Julia Scott); **35 above** Sunniva Harte (Courtney Cottage); **35 below** S & O Mathews (Graveye Manor); **36** Andrew Lawson; **36-37** S & O Mathews (Sir Harold Hillier Gardens); **37 below** Christian Sarramon (Place de las Carreras); **38** Tim Beddow/The Interior Archive (Mirella Riooiardi); **39** Christopher Simon Sykes/The Interior Archive; **40 above** Fritz von der Schulenburg/The Interior Archive (Mimmi O'Connell); **40 below** Gary Rogers/Petra Pelz; **41** Gary Rogers; **42 above** Clive Nichols(Netherfield Herb Garden); **42 below** Gary Rogers/Friedrich Carl Meyer (Henk Weijers); **43** Tom Leighton/IPC magazines; **44 above** Clive Nichols (Wollerton Old Hall, Shropshire); **44 below** Gary Rogers/Rosemary Verey, Barnsley House; **45 left** S & O Mathews (Clinton Lodge); **45 right** Deidi von Schaewen; **46** Gary Rogers/Barbara Hammerstein, Garmish-Partenkirken; **46-47** Harpur Garden Library(Cary Walinsky); **47 right** Gary Rogers/Lassalle; **47 above** John Glover (Factory Cottge, Suffolk); **48 left** Simon Kenny/Arcaid/Belle; **48-49** Harpur Garden Library(Carl Neels, Dallas); **49 right** Robin Mathews/Homes & Gardens/IPC magazines; **50 above** Leigh Clapp (Mount Wilson); **50 below** Deidi von Schaewen; **51** Gary Rogers; **52** Marijke Heuff/The Garden Picture Library(Mien Ruys Garden); **53 above** Ron Sutherland/The Garden Picture Library (Max Koch Garden); **53 below left** John Glover; **53 below right** Clive Nichols (Olivia Clarke); **54 left** Deidi von Schaewen (Chaumont); **54 right** Mayer/Le Scanff/The Garden Picture Library (Chaumont); **55** Edina van der Wyck/The Interior Archive (Anne Hatch); **56 above** S & O Mathews (Old Place Farm); **56 below** Juliette Wade (Thorpe Hall); **57** J C Mayer – G Le Scanff (Jardin de Talos); **58** Simon McBride/Homes & Gardens/IPC magazines; **59 above** Janet Sorrel/The Garden Picture Library; **59 below** Harpur Garden Library (M Hillier); **60 left** Juliette Wade (Thorpe Hall); **60 right** Simon McBride/The Interior Archive (Jilly Hopton); **61** J C Mayer – G Le Scanff (Jardin de Talos); **62 left** Ron Sutherland/The Garden Picture Library; **62-63** Harpur Garden Library (Wesley & Susan Dixon); **63 above** Harpur Garden Library (Rick Mosbaugh, Los Angeles); **63 below** Ron Sutherland/The Garden Picture Library (Anthony Paul Design); **64 above** Eduardo Munoz/The Interior Archive (Paco Munoz); **64 below** Eduardo Munoz/The Interior Archive (Mary Melian); **65** S & O Mathews (Stitches Farm House); **66-67** S & O Mathews; **67 right** Brian Carter/The Garden Picture Library; **67 above** Bill Coster/Natural History Photographic Agency; **68** S & O Mathews (Denmans, Sussex); **68-69** S & O Mathews (Brookwell, Surrey); **69 above** Mark Bolton The Garden Picture Library (Darkey Pang Tso Gang); **69 below** Jacqui Hurst/The Garden Picture Library (The Old Stones); **70** Harpur Garden Library (Ryoan-Ji Temple); **71** Harpur Garden Library (Terry Welch, Seattle); **72** Marianne Majerus (Japanese Garden, Notts); **73** Marianne Majerus(Japanese Garden, Notts); **74** Mark Bolton/The Garden Picture Library; **75** Sylvie Becquet/ Chombart de Lauwe Marie Claire Idees; **76** John Glover; **76** Leigh Clapp/Conran Octopus (Michael Cooke); **77** Andrew Lawson (Anthony Noel); **80** Juliette Wade/Conran Octopus (Cheryl Cummings); **88** Harpur Garden Library(Terence Conran); **89** Tim Clinch/The Interior Archive(Mario Connio); **90 above** Fritz von der Schulenburg/The Interior Archive (Barefoot Elegance); **90 below** Harpur Garden Library (Oehme & van Sweden/Rosenberg); **91** Zara McCalmont/The Garden Picture Library(Gregson Garden); **92** Andreas von Einsiedel/Country Homes & Interiors/IPC magazines; **93** Brigitte Thomas/ The Garden Picture Library; **94** Gary Rogers/ Stumpf; **95** Leigh Clapp; **96-97** Leigh Clapp/Conran Octopus (Michael Cooke); **98** Tim Clinch/The Interior Archive (Kate Dyson); **99** Simon Upton/The Interior Archive (Anthony Collett); **100-101** Herbert Ypma/ The Interior Archive (American Country); **101 below** Harpur Garden Library (Keith Geller, Seattle); **102-103** Harpur Garden Library (Oehme & van Sweden); **104** Harpur Garden Library; **105** Harpur Garden Library(Stephen Crisp); **106-107** Harpur Garden Library; **107 right** Harpur Garden Library (Martina Barzi & Josefine Casares); **107 below** Deidi von Schaewen (A Putman); **108** Gary Rogers/Friedrich Carl Meyer (Henk Weijers); **108-109** Hotze Eisma/Taverne (Production Hanna Poli); **110** Tim Beddow/The Interior Archive (Mirella Ricciardi); **110-111** Simon Upton/ The Interior Archive (Anthony Collett); **111 right** Eric Crichton/The Garden Picture Library; **112** Gary Rogers/Barbara Hammerstein, Garmish-Partenkirken; **113** Henry Wilson/ The Interior Archive (Anouska Hempel); **114** Harpur Garden Library (Victor Nelson); **115 left** Gary Rogers/Dammers; **115 right** Clive Nichols (Garden and Security Lighting); **116 left** Clive Nichols; **116-117** Georgie Cole/ Vogue Entertaining & Travel; **117 above right** Sylvie Becquet/ Marie-Paule Fawe/ Marie Claire Idees; **117 below left** Harpur Garden Library (Villa Bebek, Bali); **117 below right** Camera Press/Jahreszeiten-Verlag; **118** Simon Brown/The Interior Archive; **118-119** Deidi von Schaewen (Quentin); **120** Vogue Entertaining & Travel (William Meppem); **120-121** Camera Press/ Fair Lady; **122 left** Harpur Garden Library (Robert Chittock, Seattle); **122 right** Maura McEvoy; **122-123** Jerome Darblay/INSIDE; **123 right** Richard Imrie; **124 left** Tim Beddow/The Interior Archive (Emma Fole); **124 right** Debbi Treloar/Homes & Gardens/ IPC magazines; **125 left** Debbi Treloar/ Homes & Gardens/IPC magazines; **125 right** John Millar/The Garden Picture Library; **126 above** Simon Brown/The Interior Archive; **126 centre** Fritz von der Schulenburg/The Interior Archive (Anouska Hempel); **126 below** Deidi von Schaewen; **127** Steven Wooster/The Garden Picture Library (Marshall Cook Design); **128 left** Harpur Garden Library (Keeyla Meadows); **128 main picture** Gilles de Chabaneix/ Catherine Ardowin/Marie Claire Maison; **128 below** Richard Imrie; **129** Richard Imrie; **130** Camera Press/Schoner Wohnen; **130-131** Camera Press/Schoner Wohnen; **131 right** Camera Press/Schoner Wohnen; **131 centre** Camera Press/Schoner Wohnen; **132-133** Polly Wreford/Homes & Gardens/IPC magazines; **133** Jonathan Pilkington/The Interior Archive (Larraine Kirk); **134 above** Victoria Pearson/Freshstock USA; **134 below** Marie Claire Maison; **135 above** Victoria Pearson/ Freshstock USA; **136-137** Conran Octopus/ Juliette Wade (Richard Key); **138 above** Linda Burgess/Garden Picture Library; **138 below** Richard Imrie; **139** The Garden Picture Library;**140** Conran Octopus/Tim Beddow (Katherine Ireland); **144** Mark Bolton/Conran Octopus(Julie Toll); **148** Simon Brown; **149** Simon Brown; **150 above** Richard Imrie; **150 below** Conran Octopus/ Richard Imrie; **151** Conran Octopus/Richard Imrie; **152** Richard Imrie; **153 above left** Richard Imrie; **153 above right** Richard Imrie; **153 below** Clive Nichols/ Nichols Garden, Reading; **154** Conran Octopus/ Marianne Majerus (Elton Hall, Herefordshire); **154-155** Marianne Majerus (Tom Stuart-Smith); **155** Homes & Gardens/ IPC Syndication; **156 above** Curtice Taylor (Heaton-Renshaw); **156 below** Leigh Clapp/ Conran Octopus (Michael Cooke); **157** John Glover (Monkswood, Surrey); **158-159** Gary Rogers (Henk Weijers); **159 right** Tim Beddow/The Interior Archive (Emma Fole); **160 left** Conran Octopus/Juliette Wade; **160 above** Caroline Arber For Dulux Colour Magazine; **160 below** Caroline Arber For Dulux Colour Magazine; **161 above** Tim Beddow/The Interior Archive (Kathryn Ireland); **161 below** Clive Nichols/Nichols Garden, Reading; **162 above left** Conran Octopus/Richard Imrie; **162 above right** Richard Imrie; **162 below right** IPC magazines/ Homes & Gardens/Trevor Richards; **162-163** Leigh Clapp; **164 left** Richard Imrie; **164 right** Sunniva Harte (Courtney Cottage); **165** Gary Rogers (Henk Weijers); **166 left** Earl Carter; **166 above** Richard Imrie; **166 below** Juliette Wade; **167 left** Andrew Lawson; **167 right** Juliette Wade; **168 left** Richard Imrie; **168 right** Juliette Wade; **168 above** Marianne Majerus (George Carter); **169** Gary Rogers; **170 above left** S & O Mathews(Roselle Close, Hants); **170 above right** Conran Octopus/JulietteWade (Richard Key); **170 below** Tim Goffe/Paxton Locker Architects; **171 above left** Leigh Clapp/Conran Octopus (Michael Cooke); **171 above right** VNU Syndication (Eric van Lokven); **171 below left** Leigh Clapp/ Conran Octopus (Michael Cooke); **171 below right** Leigh Clapp/Conran Octopus (Michael Cooke); **172 left** Kudos Features Ltd (Brian Harrison); **172-173** Conran Octopus/Tim Beddow (Katherine Ireland); **173 above right** Leigh Clapp; **173 below right** Conran Octopus/Marianne Majerus (Elton Hall, Herefordshire); **174** Curtis Taylor; **175** Garden Picture Library **176** Conran Octopus/Juliette Wade; **178 above left** Marie Claire Idees; **178 below left** Marie Claire Idees; **192** Conran Octopus/ Richard Imrie.

The following photographs were specially taken for Conran Octopus: Tim Beddow courtesy of Kathryn Ireland 140-143; Mark Bolton courtesy of Clive and Joy(garden design by Julie Toll) 144-147; Leigh Clapp courtesy Michael Cooke(owner and designer) and family 80-83; Marianne Majerus courtesy of Elton Hall with special thanks to Puffin and Pelican, Anthony Brooks, Ted Wade and Caroline Hainsworth 184-187; Juliette Wade courtesy of Monica Bohn-Duchen and family 180-183; Juliette Wade courtesy of Cheryl Cummings owner and garden designer 84-87.

Every effort has been made to trace the copyright holders. We apologise in advance for any unintentional omission, and would be pleased to insert the appropriate acknowledgement in any subsequent edition.

index

Page numbers in *italics* refer to photographs